The Curiosities of British Children's TV

BEN RICKETTS

Copyright © 2017 Ben Ricketts

Cover designed by Markus (www.markustudio.com)

All rights reserved. This book or any portion thereof may not be reproduced or used in any manner whatsoever without the express written permission of the publisher.

ISBN-13: 978-1542582391

CONTENTS

Introduction
1. Sebastian the Incredible Drawing Dog — 3
2. Jackson Pace: The Great Years — 9
3. Chips' Comic — 17
4. Earthfasts — 29
5. Clapperboard — 37
6. Break in the Sun — 43
7. Hokey Cokey — 49
8. Tales from Fat Tulip's Garden — 54
9. Chock-a-Block — 62
10. The Pig Attraction — 68
11. Teddy Edward — 75
12. Mop and Smiff — 81
13. Running Scared — 88
14. Let's Pretend — 95
15. Alfonso Bonzo — 105
16. Bric-a-Brac — 110
17. Round the Bend — 114
18. Orm and Cheep — 125
19. Codename Icarus — 129
20. Heggerty Haggerty — 136
21. Behind the Bike Sheds — 141
22. Over the Moon — 151
23. Ragdolly Anna — 158
24. Zokko! — 163
25. Get Up and Go! / Mooncat & Co — 171
Acknowledgements

INTRODUCTION

Children's TV holds a special place in everyone's heart. It's our first experience of a medium which will go on to have a huge cultural significance in our lives, so the memories of these formative years are fondly remembered. And that's why, all these years on, we're still talking about *Bagpuss, Camberwick Green, Rainbow* et al.

There's a primitive simplicity to these older shows, particularly when compared to the flashy brilliance of modern children's TV budgets. Harking back to more innocent times, there's a warm and pleasing fuzz of nostalgia attached to discussing these classic slices of children's TV, so it's no surprise that people are so ready to discuss them.

However, you know what? There's absolutely nothing else that can be said about Zammo tainting *Grange Hill* with heroin, not one more word that can be written about *Captain Pugwash's* completely imaginary mate Seaman Staines and there's most certainly no more time for a celebrity talking head to sing the theme tune to *Trap Door*. It's time for something a little different, but what?

The landscape of British children's TV is a varied frontier and one where certain shows – for many reasons – have slipped through the fragile cracks in our memories and are now less than represented in the collective consciousness or, if they are, they're memories which have been distorted beyond all recognition.

And that's why I decided to track down some of these oddities (and the people behind them) in order to not only rediscover some intriguing corners of British children's TV, but also bring our memories up to date and tell the whole truth behind these shows. It all started on my blog (www.curiousbritishtelly.co.uk) and this quest has now spilled into the pages of this book.

SEBASTIAN THE INCREDIBLE DRAWING DOG

BBC1
1986

Venture into any house containing small children and you're bound to find oodles of drawings. Sure, most children's efforts involve out of proportion heads balancing upon two stick legs, but the effort's there, right? And it's a fine outlet for their imagination and creativity to run wild, so it should never be stymied.

Now, children *also* love pets. They're equals, in a sense, as they're ruled by their adult parents/owners, so it's no surprise they strike up such great relationships. And with similar centres of gravity, children and dogs make for excellent playmates. Their relationships may seem nothing more than frivolous larks, but they actually help nurture a child's social development.

What about a TV show, then, which married art and dogs? Sounding custom built for success, it actually happened back in 1986. And throwing a young Michael Barrymore into the mix surely meant that *Sebastian the Incredible Drawing Dog* was destined for tremendous success, right?

The Importance of Being Sebastian

Surrounded by archaic clutter in a dimly lit flat, Sebastian (operated by Richard Robinson) expresses his furry musings through the medium of paint and canvas. To ensure that the fine relationship between man and dog is maintained, Michael (Michael Barrymore) also lives there, presumably to arrange visits to the vet and remove ticks from the more unreachable parts of Sebastian's shaggy anatomy.

Michael, unable to match Sebastian's artistic temperament, finds himself larking about round the flat instead. One day, Michael may be dressing up as Lord Nelson, the next he might be searching for a pair of socks. A chance comment on these nonsensical meanderings soon leads to Michael dusting down the 'large and unusual storybook'. From this, Michael regales viewers with a quirky tale as Sebastian provides the illustrations.

Sketching Sebastian

Sebastian first bounded onto our screens in 1986 and a total of 13 five minute episodes aired on BBC1 in the Children's BBC afternoon slot. The series was the brainchild of writer and cartoonist, David Myers, who had previously written for Dave Allen and Tommy Cooper.

David Myers produced an early pilot of *Sebastian* with Pic Productions, but the final series would be a BBC production helmed by Christopher Pilkington who had previously produced the children's TV shows *Hartbeat* and *Captain Zep – Space Detective*. Later on in the 1990s, Pilkington would before going on to act as the executive producer for numerous Children's BBC shows.

Repeats of *Sebastian* aired throughout 1987 and 1988 on BBC1 and BBC2, but this was the last the world saw of *Sebastian*. Nonetheless, the series' managed to maintain a permanent presence in the physical world thanks to a series of books published by Andre Deutsch Ltd in 1987 which were written and illustrated by David Myers

On the Quest for Sebastian

Sebastian was an enigmatic presence in my life for the good part of two and a half decades. The lingering image of a dog in a smoking jacket was embedded deep within my memory and frequently bubbled to the surface, prompting me to question my memory under an intense spotlight.

I had to find out more about the series, but the problem was that no one else remembered it. And I certainly couldn't recall the title, having been barely old enough to remember my own name at the time.

Rather fortuitously, many years on, I found myself confronted with a 1986 issue of the Radio Times – Russ Abbot was on the cover, so how could I resist picking it up? It was an amazing trip down memory lane, but the real sweetener lay towards the back of the issue. There was an article in there about some new show featuring Michael Barrymore entitled *Sebastian the Incredible Drawing Dog*.

Finally, I had the name of this elusive show in my grasp! I immediately hopped online to see what I could discover, but all I found were half-truths and whispers. Unfortunately, it appeared that this show was *completely* forgotten. Many men would have floundered in this situation, but I was determined to squeeze a few more drops of nostalgia juice out of my grey matter. So, with a new found sense of purpose, I headed for the BFI Archive.

The BFI Archive is to TV history enthusiasts as the Black Stone of Mecca is to Muslims. Visiting this underground viewing archive is something that every TV anorak needs to do at least once in their life. It helps you to achieve a better spiritual enlightenment and, more importantly, watch some really rare television.

The viewing rooms are housed in what can only be described as a series of subterranean caverns. And, yes, scrambling through all the old VHS tapes and film cans, you do find yourself feeling a bit like a Womble. However, whereas Orinoco sought to recycle rubbish, I was seeking to remind the world of *Sebastian*. It was time to get started, so I pressed the play button on the BFI's dusty VHS player and got stuck in.

Sebastian is a particularly cultured dog; instead of inquisitively sniffing other dog's rectums, he's much more at home playing the violin or piano and, of course, he's a dab hand with the old paintbrush bristles. Naturally, this high level of sophistication hints at a privileged background, so it's no surprise to discover he's a well-spoken hound. And this aristocratic air is further evidenced by a pith helmet which hangs on a hatstand and no doubt saw plenty of action in the old empire.

Barrymore, meanwhile, is positioned as the funny man to Sebastian's straight man (dog) and old Michael bounds onto the screen like a cartoon kangaroo let loose amongst the under 7s. Winking and smiling with all the engaging grace of the very best frontmen, Barrymore demonstrates his precious talent with an electric performance which refuses to be tainted by his disturbingly bland 1980s jumpers.

It's interesting to note that *Sebastian* began airing just a few weeks before the first series of *Strike it Lucky*, so it truly finds Barrymore teetering on the precipice of greatness.

And it's Barrymore's exhilarating personality that helps to dictate the show's main strength – the relationship between Michael and Sebastian. They bicker, squabble and banter amongst themselves with a striking dichotomy which recalls all the best double acts.

Barrymore simply thrives on having someone to bounce off; it's what his personality gets up for in the morning. Sebastian, meanwhile, with his air of debonair sophistication, provides a fantastic foil for our zany boy from Bermondsey.

One moment, Barrymore may be hamming it up as a pirate whilst he poses for Sebastian's Treasure Island painting, but this frivolity is soon soured when Barrymore sneezes and causes Sebastian to smudge his painting. This, in turn, leads to Sebastian's artistic pretensions erupting in a moment of fine characterisation. It's a pairing which hits that rare sweet spot of dynamics and, in that respect, achieves everything children's TV should.

This relationship sets up a marvellous structure for the show, but just as it's reaching its ascendency it begins slipping off track. As the large and unusual storybook is opened, Michael and Sebastian's outstanding chemistry is suddenly disabled.

The stories are too slight, mere whispers in the wind generated by Hurricane Barrymore. Maybe there's some hilarity to be found in discovering what's under Tall Hat Joe's hat, but it never quite feels good enough and the stories splutter home as Michael's exuberance is sharply throttled; it's a change in pace which is completely unnecessary for five-minute episodes and is an obvious thorn in the series' side.

The moribund tone of the stories is also coupled to illustrations which are barely more than black and white scribbles. David Myer was a talented cartoonist, but he's simply not given the time to let his talents shine here.

Man's Best Friend?

Blessed with a fantastic central pairing, *Sebastian* makes for an exciting spectacle and it really is a pleasure to watch Barrymore when he's on such scintillating form. Frustratingly, the format struggles to maintain that energy over the short running times due to the unfortunate speed bump that is the less than captivating stories. As it is, *Sebastian* remains flawed, but peppered with moments of real joy.

JACKSON PACE: THE GREAT YEARS

ITV
1990

The swashbuckling life of an explorer looks like a nonstop adventure packed full of drama, heroism and plenty of wisecracks. Seen through the eyes of a child it's an intoxicating mix of emotions and instinct which corrupt the very fabric of normal life.

After all, society dictates that we should get a sensible haircut and embark on the 9 – 5 grind to provide security. But, seriously, what child in their right mind wants to work towards the horror of listening to Pat in Accounts waffling on about her hysterectomy?

It's no surprise, then, to find that children absolutely love Indiana Jones as it's a thrilling franchise which serves up scene after scene of adrenaline fuelled action. Sure, the threat of malaria is always just around the corner, but it's worth the risk to avoid the banal world of 'proper grownups'.

And it's this glamorous appeal which led to a spoof of the genre in *Jackson Pace: The Great Years*.

Adventure Awaits

Jackson Pace (Keith Allen) is an adventuring dynamo who's handy with his fists, loves the glint of a precious treasure and refuses to give up on anything. All good heroes are accompanied by a trusty sidekick and Pace has Roger Whibley (Daniel Peacock) shoring up his side at all times. Pace even comes complete with a battle cry catchphrase of "There's gold to be gained!"

And this catchphrase is going to be bellowed out against a thrilling adventure based upon the parchment of Kinard. And exactly what is this parchment? Well, it's an important document which details the whereabouts of three sacred keystones.

Whoever gets their mitts on these elusive keystones is then able to unlock – take a deep breath – the mighty gates of the hidden temple in the land of Ja Ja Bar. But what lies within these mystical gates? Well no one knows, but, everyone's clamouring for it, so it must be worth a bit of adventuring.

Now, Pace and Whibley are plucky chaps, but their quest is going to be littered with all manner of villainous mercenaries. The main antagonist is Princess Layme (Cory Pulman), an Egyptian princess who hopes to use the treasure of Kinard to bankroll the construction of an opulent palace.

Layme's surrounded at all times by her snivelling assistant Lord Layta (Paul B Davies) and the blind mystic Lord Taggon (Hugh Paddick). They're also joined by the sarcastic chap The Head (Arthur Smith) – yes, he's literally a head in the sand.

Squirming around on the periphery of Layme's attentions is the weedy and bespectacled Prince Filo (Gian Sammarco). Determined to be a dashing hero – in the mould of Pace – he's desperate to bring back the treasure of Kinard and quash Pace for good. Filo is convinced this is the best way to Layme's heart, but unfortunately she views him more as a wingless fly in the ointment.

Filo may pose no tangible threat to Pace, but there's guaranteed trouble in the form of shady American, Commander Daken (Nic D'Avirro). He's the traditional 'man in black', but unlike Will Smith he has neither the dance moves nor the loveable charm. Instead, he's a ruthless killer complete with – like all the best villains – a robotic hand which wants to crush Pace's fragile neck into a million tiny pieces.

Danger is certainly breathing heavily down Pace and Whibley's necks, but they're not completely up the proverbial creek without a paddle. The resourceful journalist, Ryveeta Tusk (Josie Lawrence), has stowed away on Pace's plane to get an exclusive scoop for her tabloid rag. As to be expected, her beating Fleet Street heart means there's a certain level of self interest in her involvement, but she's the closest thing Pace has to an ally.

Together, the various factions will embark on a breathtaking series of adventures mapping the entire globe. These incredibly bizarre exploits will include meeting the lost tribe of Popapa, swinging through the jungle with Tarzan, nearly becoming Barry the Yeti's dinner and being forced to endure the hideous culinary delights of the Fat Lady.

On the Trail

Six episodes of *Jackson Pace* aired in 1990 on ITV and the series was created by Daniel Peacock. *Jackson Pace* was the first TV script penned by Peacock and stemmed from his love of Indiana Jones as he recalls:

"Indiana Jones had just come out and I really liked it. I thought 'Why don't I see if I can get some comedy out of this' and I did. I thought it was a funny idea so I went to see Nick Wilson – head of children's TV at Granada – and he said 'Give me six', so I did!"

These six episodes were directed by Alistair Clark who arrived at *Jackson Pace* with an excellent CV which took in *Grange Hill*, *Children's Ward* and *No. 73*. This impressive foundation needed a stunning cast and, thanks to the connections of producer Mark Robson, it received a cast crowded with comedy stars. The stage was set for something very special to emerge, but what would the viewing public think of *Jackson Pace?*

Well, the viewing figures were highly respectable with around 4 million people tuning into each episode. Despite this success the series was never repeated. Peacock had hoped that there would be a second series and left it open with the possibility of 'Pace in Space', but for reasons unknown this never materialised. To compound this frustration even further there has never been a commercial release or repeat of *Jackson Pace*. Peacock interprets this as:

"Television was very different then to how it is now. They made a show and once it was broadcast that was that, especially on children's TV at the time. And, despite the extraordinary viewing figures, maybe they didn't know where to place it. I'd love to see a DVD release, but when Granada went down it all became very complicated"

Setting the Pace

Back in 1990, I watched *Jackson Pace* and it was easily my most favourite TV show in the world at the time. I was so smitten with it that I hatched a plan to invite Jackson Pace himself round for a cup of tea. Sadly, my Mum wasn't too keen on this idea and, instead, encouraged me to simply enjoy the show.

Despite my obsession with the series, I couldn't remember the name of it. Sure, I remembered that it featured some explorer chap and, yeah, he had a catchphrase about gold, but could I remember what this mysterious show was? No!

Drawing nothing but blank after blank, I resigned myself to never rediscovering it. Then, out of the blue, someone contacted me through my blog and said "Do you remember *Jackson Pace: The Great Years?* It's about this Indiana Jones style adventurer..."

And, before I knew it, I was down at the BFI Archive.

There's Gold to be Gained!

The most immediate factor to strike me was the appearance of Jackson Pace himself. I always remembered him being the stereotypically handsome and dashing explorer type. Rather perplexingly, my recent research had informed me that Keith Allen played Jackson Pace.

Now, don't get me wrong, Keith Allen's a good looking chap, but I wouldn't associate him with the charismatic good looks of a rugged hero. However, put him in a leather jacket with a full head of long, lustrous hair and he's actually rather tasty!

Once I'd managed to control my burgeoning man crush for Keith Allen, it was time to evaluate the action. And to say it took my breath away would be an understatement. *Jackson Pace* is simply bursting at the seams with scene after scene of manic action.

Daniel Peacock could have taken the opportunity to communicate some deep messages about man's desire to ransack the world of its native treasures, but that wouldn't be much fun, would it? Instead he's gone for a deliberate pace which is balls out entertainment.

And *Jackson Pace* is a lampoon which absolutely lets rip on the *Indiana Jones* series. Not content with lifting the fantastically hokey sacred stones straight out of *Temple of Doom*, Peacock makes sure that plenty of other targets are in his sights. That's why we get the quintessential punch up in a Cairo nightclub, jungle scenes swarming with danger, Ryveeta Tusk as the natural successor to Willie Scott and the obigatory fight atop a moving train. And all these staples of adventure are delivered at a breakneck speed as the action zips from one far flung location to another.

But the only way you can do justice to such action is if you have a first-rate cast in place. Rest assured, *Jackson Pace* does not disappoint in this respect. It's difficult to single anyone out due to the string of performances delivered with such infectious, anarchic energy. In fact, the only way to describe the cast list is to say it feels like you've walked into The Comedy Store on a particularly manic night in the 1980s. Peacock has fond memories of the cast and the production:

"The majority of the cast came from the producer Mark Robson. I knew Keith, but most of the casting was down to Mark. I liked all these – at the time – young, fresh faces and wanted to put together a team of very funny people. And it was very funny on set, people would chip in with ideas and, if they weren't funny, I immediately rejected them! The real fun, however, came in the bar afterwards where we used to do singsongs and things like that!"

And this raucous fun translates into the scripts which are wrapped up in razor sharp gags. Frankly, it would be difficult for a jury to convict the series of anything less than first degree hilarity. The humour being machine gunned out is also astounding due to its adult nature. I couldn't believe that a Children's ITV show was able to slip in (ahem) references to boobies, school boy masturbation and Josie Lawrence munching seductively upon a sausage (enough to give any man palpitations). I asked Peacock how difficult it was to get this on screen and he explained:

"No, there were no problems at all. To be honest, I wrote it and I didn't even think they might cut it. And they didn't cut it. It was there to be humorous and Granada, at the time, were very good. They didn't bat an eyelid"

Perhaps it's the type of humour which, if handled incorrectly, could be seen as a corrupting influence. When it's delivered with a joyous, childlike energy, it would be a crime to try and tame it. And, as my session at the BFI came to an end, I realised that, in the last 25 years, it hadn't done me any harm.

Mission Complete

I absolutely loved catching up with *Jackson Pace*. It was exciting, it was fabulous and I frankly couldn't get enough of its hilarious rough and tumble charm. Somehow it remains curiously forgotten and obscured by the shimmering haze of much more successful shows. I guess that it's actually possible for the margins of TV magnificence to be truly stretched, but still fail to leave an indelible mark on its history.

A show like *Maid Marian and Her Merry Men* is probably the closest equal to *Jackson Pace* in terms of style, tone and quality. However, *Maid Marian* is leagues ahead in terms of recognition as it was gifted those most coveted commodities in television – re-commissions and repeats. *Jackson Pace* never received these vital leg-ups, so it failed to keep the ball rolling and hone its reputation as a glorious example of British children's TV. To those who remember it, the rigours of time will never diminish its splendour.

And if Keith Allen's reading then I still want you to come round mine for a cup of tea. I've got my own place now, so my Mum can't stop me.

CHIPS' COMIC

Channel 4
1983 - 84

If you were to take a cursory glance across my bedroom as a child, in amongst all the bootleg action figures from PoundStretcher and chewed upon pieces of Lego, you would find piles and piles of comics. Children, you see, absolutely love comics and comics love them.

A marvellous conduit for early introductions to narratives and humour, comics are packed full of features on the world to delight and challenge that developing cerebral cortex. It's a deceptively educative packaging of fun and one which has remained popular for well over a century.

Now, to a young child, putting a comic together may sound like a dream job bursting with japes and fun, but is it actually all illustrator strikes and paper shortages? Well, no, it's actually all japes and fun as evidenced in the process of putting together *Chips' Comic*.

Comic Strips and Chips

Inky (Gordon Griffin) and Elsa (Elsa O'Toole) have decided that it's time to start a new comic; being the early 1980s, the only way to get anything done is through the magic of an 8 bit computer, so this is where Inky and Elsa enlist the help of Chips.

A huge, yellow behemoth of a computer, Chips is a curious concoction of monitors, coat hanger aerials, flashing lights and levers. Living within Chips' digital belly are the blocky computer men, Smasher and Basher who help to demonstrate various puzzles and animations. Oh, and Chips' abilities even stretch to making drinks and toast, so there's little doubt of his value to the team.

The team, however, isn't complete until the arrival of its final member. Rover (Andrew Secombe) is a bipedal dog whose tragic background has seen him kicked out of his previous owner's house. Luckily, he turns up at Inky and Elsa's and despite the initial language difficulties (Rover can only communicate through mime), they decide to take him in.

Together, this group look at themes such as water, life underground, morning, night time and rainbows to help form the basis of individual issues of Chips' Comic. With the structure of a theme in place, it's up to Inky, Elsa, Rover and Chips' to create the features for the comic and these are neatly delivered by a number of specialist pages.

The 'Do It Yourself' page usually finds one of the team getting to grips with an activity e.g. setting an alarm clock. The 'Puzzle' page tests the viewers' knowledge on subjects such as which plant foods grow above or below the ground. The 'Animal' page decides to investigate subjects such as where milk comes from. The 'Poetry' and 'Story' pages are fairly self-explanatory and, finally, 'Rover's Report' finds Rover going out into the world on his motorbike to visit balloon factories or, through the power of green screen, the rainforest.

With all of this information uploaded into Chips – as long as he isn't busy making drinks – production of the comic can start once Inky has pulled all the right levers. And, the true beauty of *Chips' Comic* is that the comic produced is then available in all good newsagents for the viewer to buy.

Drafting the Comic

Chips' Comic consisted of two series of 10 episodes which were 25 minutes long and aired on Channel 4 in 1983 and 1984. The first series was transmitted at 5.30pm on Wednesday evenings whereas the second series went out at 1.30pm on Saturday afternoons. Channel 4 repeated the series up until 1985, but repeats were still aired on Welsh language channel S4C as late as 1987.

Mo Harter acted as producer on the series with children's playwright David Wood in the role of producer. The series – originally touted as *Comput-a-Comic* – was produced by Verronmead in association with Primetime Television and was the first slice of original children's programming for Channel 4. The initial inklings of the series came, like all the best ideas, from a need to advance what television was capable of as Mo Harter explains:

"I witnessed the fascination TV held for children, my own son in particular, and felt it could be developed more positively, including learning, entertainment, involvement, music, be inclusive of a wider range of children and of mixed abilities. My son, Matthew, had learning difficulties and it was clear that television was a resource that was not serving him, or children like him.

I had been inspired by 'Vision On', a predominantly visual programme which held the attention of both deaf and hearing children with its strong visual appeal. I then took my children to see a play by David Wood and felt he had a way of capturing and holding the attention of children whilst entertaining them. I approached him hoping he might be interested in developing a children's TV series and he was"

David Wood remembers being intrigued by Harter's vision and keen to investigate getting the show off the ground:

"The fact that I had performed in children's programmes for the BBC, including Play Away and Jackanory, meant that I knew a little about children's TV programming, and quite fancied the idea of becoming involved in Mo's project.

But, to be honest, I wasn't sure that we stood a chance of creating something that the BBC or ITV would be interested in. It was really the announcement that Channel 4 was starting up, with a brief to employ independent producers, that spurred us on. Other people came on board as advisers and creative contributors, and soon the dream became a reality"

A strong formula was required for the series to meet Harter's aspirations and achieve everything required, so the team quickly got to work as she explains:

"David developed the format and we then involved an Educational Adviser and a children's illustrator. We adopted the underlying principles of good communication – ideas presented with a strong visual appeal, reinforced with music, puzzles, rhyme, the fun of finding out about things, doing it yourself etc – each programme had a strong theme.

I believe the educational word was 'schematic'. My own research revealed that very few ideas could be learned or understood by a children's audience in one programme). We presented one or two and reinforced them with music, humour, visuals, poems etc"

Helping to bring further life and colour to the series' concept was Jan Pienkowski who was already known to practically every child in land. Woods had previously worked with Pienkowski and was keen to get him on board:

"Jan, of course, was well known as the illustrator/co-creator of the Meg And Mog books and novelty books like The Haunted House. I had written and directed the stage version of Meg And Mog, so, with Mo's blessing, invited Jan to contribute graphics and video idents for the show. At the time these were quite advanced for television!"

Chips' Comic wouldn't be *Chips' Comic* without the physical comic that viewers could go and buy, so it's a central part of the series' story. The comics were produced alongside each series and continued for a short while afterwards. Woods came up with the idea to tie the series' ethos in with a physical comic, but he concedes that it wasn't necessarily the easiest approach to take:

"A real-life comic, available in the shops, echoing the television programme, week by week, was an idea that we soon realised would be very difficult to achieve. For one thing, the production deadlines for television and for the publishing of a comic are totally different.

We had to provide the material for the comic long before we recorded the television programme. This meant that we had to commit to the programme content way in advance. Sometimes, not very often, an item would have to be cut from the programme, but would then later turn up in the comic!

Having a printed version of the programme was all part and parcel of the educational aims. The comic, in the hands of a child with, or without, learning difficulties, would reinforce the content seen on the programme, and perhaps encourage the child to look and read and assimilate more than was possible from just one viewing of the programme.

We talked to various people before becoming involved with IPC, a major producer of comics and magazines. We enjoyed our association with them, and they made every effort to be faithful to the characters and ideas in the programme, finding inventive ways of adapting them for the printed page"

Helping to tie the content and comic together was the music which was provided by the musician and composer duo of Juliet Lawson and Peter Hope. Picking up the story, Juliet Lawson looks back at how she got involved in the series:

"In the 1980's I was writing songs with a musical arranger, Peter Hope, and we were asked to submit a demo tape of possible songs for a new children's programme that Channel 4 were making. We had a rather eccentric meeting in a cafe at Waterloo Station with all creative contributors offering up their ideas and Peter and me humming embryonic tunes as a sort of starting point.

Peter's and my brief was simply that each episode would be themed (where does petrol come from, getting dressed, keeping your room tidy, fireworks, going to the sea side, visiting a farm to name a few). The producers insisted that we mustn't 'talk down' to children and the songs we came up with I think appealed to adults as well as the intended 5 - 8 years old audience that the show was aimed at"

Airing during Channel 4's infancy, *Chips' Comic* was part of an exciting new lineup which the channel hoped would define its innovative outlook on television. David Woods believes that one of the main reasons Channel 4 embraced the series was due to its educational content and the unique demographic it was aimed at:

"The educational possibilities offered by the printed comic helped considerably, I believe, in us getting the commission to make the programmes from Channel 4. At that time, Channel 4 had no children's department. We went to the Education Department (Naomi Sargant) and received a warm welcome. We thus became the first ever children's series on Channel 4. But we would never have got the commission if the programmes hadn't been educational. The comic became the equivalent of, say, accompanying teachers' notes"

And Harter remembers the early days of Channel 4 as being testing, but very exciting:

"It was very different to working with an established broadcaster – I worked for the BBC for many years. We had to find our own office, install telephones, employ staff, audition actors, find our own post-production house, director, animator, song-writers – all on hand at the BBC and if not there's a department to help you find what you want.
It felt a bit like we were making it up as we went along but it was exciting being part of creating a new freelance community of programme makers and assembling the necessary skills and talents need to make TV programmes. Channel 4 themselves were also making it up as they went along to some extent so were very supportive of us. We were in it together and co-creating something new"

Flicking Through the Pages

Chips' Comic originally aired when I was of an age that even fragments of memories were difficult enough to store, let alone fully fledged memories, so I had absolutely no recollection of the series. Sure, I may have caught a glimpse of the later repeats, but if these memories ever existed they were a stock which had been liquidated shortly afterwards.

Thankfully, one of the main benefits of running a blog devoted to the lesser known curios of British TV is that you receive plenty of tip offs regarding shows which are ensconced in a layer of nostalgic fuzz. And, following a guest article on *Chips' Comic*, by a loyal follower of my blog, my curiosity was piqued by what was one of Channel 4's early forays into original programming.

Despite an initial struggle to find any footage online, I was eventually, thanks to a combination of visits to the BFI and the donation of various episodes, able to gather together enough material to take a closer look at *Chips' Comic*.

There's an air of familiarity around the structure of *Chips' Comic* with its use of stories, songs, learning and looking at the world around us, but beneath this recognisable exterior there's the unique joy provided by being able to actually go and buy the comic being produced. Whilst it's obvious that Inky, Elsa, Rover and Chips haven't handcrafted the comics, they provide a level of interaction with the viewers that other TV shows fail to match.

And it's clear to see, from the opening scenes, that the actors involved and the chemistry between them is going to be one of the driving forces in engaging the viewers.

Gordon Griffin, who had previously appeared in David Wood's play The Owl and the Pussycat Went to See, brings plenty of experience to the series having featured in *Z-Cars, Doctor in the House* and *When the Boat Comes In*. Never short of comic shrewdness, Griffin gifts a highly likeable air to Inky as the cheerful handyman – even if he's prone to exclaiming "Sprockets!" which appears to be the series' take on swearing fed through the filter of children's TV!

Elsa O'Toole, meanwhile, arrives in *Chip's Comic* straight out of training from the Bristol Old Vic Theatre School; recalling how new to the whole auditioning lark she was, Elsa even ended up helping David Wood and Mo Harter clear away the chairs after her audition. Nonetheless, Elsa – all dressed in wondrous 80s jumpsuits and headbands – brings a professional manner to the series to create a big sister character who is blessed with a fantastic singing voice.

With a Goon for a father, it's no surprise to discover that Andy Secombe has inherited the comedy gene and his performance in *Chips' Comic* digs deep into this DNA for a remarkable performance. Mime is never an easy art form to handle, but Secombe manages to blend articulate facial expressions and pronounced physical movements with an impeccable slickness. And all whilst wearing a suit which must have left him sweltering under the harsh glare of the studio lights.

Woods had previously worked with Secombe and knew he would be right for the role:

"Andy had worked for me in both The Owl And The Pussycat Went To See... *and* The Gingerbread Man. *He had played the title role in* The Gingerbread Man *at the Old Vic. He had a warm and endearing personality, reminiscent of his father, the great Harry Secombe, sang well and was a great physical performer"*

O'Toole has warm memories of working not just with her fellow actors, but also the team behind the camera:

"Gordon and I got on like a house on fire, I fell for his dry Geordie wit and ready quips from the first day we worked together...we're still in

contact! Gordon knew it was my first TV job and he was a real champ, always so kind and supportive of me.

One of the most standout memories, without hesitation, would have to be working with David Wood and Mo Harter, all kind-hearted, huge fun to work with – we never had a cross word and I'm happy to say, we're still in touch…they made it a wonderful experience. I just hope that David and Mo have forgiven the giggling fits, Gordon and I did have a few!"

Griffin has similarly happy memories of his time working on the series:

"It was very important of course that the three of us got on. And we did. We became friends and I'm still in touch with both Elsa and Andy. The show looks fairly simple and straightforward but they were quite hard work. We worked long hours, but it was great fun.

I remember looking forward to rehearsals and trying out all the ideas. It was a very happy show to do. In a very long and busy career, I look back on Chips' Comic fondly as one of my most enjoyable jobs"

These superb dynamics are complemented by the quality of the content which allows the series to easily sidestep any accusations of being children's TV by numbers.

Naturally, features such as the Puzzle page and the Do It Yourself page may, to an adult, appear to lack complexity, but for children they represent understandable learning with a rewarding payoff. And this can be as simple as learning about alarm clocks with a fun, shaggy dog or discovering how you can create a rainbow with felt tip pens.

Children, however, are wide eyed little beings ready to absorb all about the world around them, so Rover's Report is surely one of the most appealing features of *Chips' Comic*. And, I'm not going to lie, even in my mid 30s I find them fascinating; who, for example, knew how balloons or felt tip pens were made? *Chips' Comic*, though, provides this knowledge with visits to the respective factories.

And, as for the visit to long defunct supermarket chain, Fine Fare, it presents a fantastic time capsule of shopping in the early 1980s jam-packed with retro products, advertising and even a punk doing his weekly shop.

Providing the soundtrack for all this content, the music is one of the series' finest achievements and allows it to bathe in a melodic greatness. The brilliant theme tune is all honky tonk piano and lyrics about clapping your hands and turning pages, but the true magnificence is found within the songs of the main section. Juliet Lawson and Peter Hope have crafted songs which, for children's TV, have highly complex arrangements behind lyrics about the simple aspects of life. They're fascinating compositions and exhibit the vast experience the pair bring to the series.

Accompanying the music, *Chips' Comic* also comes loaded with a number of appealing visuals. Most eye-catching is Chips, who appears to be a distant cousin of the computer in *Chock-a-Block*, but with more personality.

And, in an era when many children's TV shows were set in sparse studios, the series' hand drawn black and white backgrounds (with strategically placed Meg and Mog books) are a more interesting setting than one relying on budget enforced minimalism. Crucially, these visuals act as the final piece in the jigsaw to ensure that the charm of *Chips' Comic* is firmly in place.

After two series, countless comics, annuals and a

book/cassette combination, time was called on *Chips' Comic* and this is somewhat of a shame as I genuinely believe there were still plenty of topics to explore and, more importantly, fun to have with the characters. Harter remembers talks with Channel 4 about a third series, but unfortunately it never advanced beyond the discussion stage.

Worth a Read?

Back in the 1980s, new TV channels were an extremely rare phenomenon and, accordingly, this meant that when Channel 4 launched in 1982 it was the subject of intense interest.

Getting off to a sublime start with its first ever show being *Countdown,* Channel 4 was able to maintain this run of form with *Chips' Comic.* It's a series which encapsulates everything that children's TV does so well: a remarkable combination of cast chemistry, innovative approaches to learning and, most importantly, a sense of fun and exploration which is clean, focused and hard to beat.

EARTHFASTS

BBC1
1994

Adults struggle to cope with the stresses and pitfalls of life, so God knows how children manage to cope with concepts such as loss and displacement. It's the inability to have any sense of control in these situations which is most frustrating and can cause soaring levels of angst.

However, throughout childhood, there's a general learning process by which you begin to understand the world around you a little bit better. And, along the way, you'll also learn how to handle the testing challenges of time slips, mischievous spirits and giant stone men marching across the landscape. Well, uh, at least that's what you'd gather from watching *Earthfasts*.

The Mystery of the Stones

Pootling around on a desolate hillside – populated by nothing but a curious collection of ancient standing stones – Keith (Chris Downs) and David (Paul Nicholls) are investigating the apparent movement of said stones and an ominous rumbling sound which has been troubling Keith.

Tracking the rumbling sound to a rock face jutting out of a hillside, Keith and David's understanding of the physical and spiritual world is put through the wringer when the rock face parts; emerging from the hillside's dark belly is 18th century drummer boy Nellie Jack John (Bryan Dick).

Accompanied by an ever flickering – yet strangely cold –

candle, Nellie Jack John reveals that only minutes earlier he had entered the hillside in search of King Arthur's ancient treasure. And Nellie Jack John is most dismissive of Keith and David's protestations that it's 1993. Confused and frustrated by his displacement, Nellie Jack John eventually marches back into the hillside, but, by now, life is becoming even stranger for Keith and David.

A mysterious spirit known as a boggart is kicking up all sorts of bad behaviour at a local cottage, huge swathes of pigs are going missing, standing stones are coming to life and Nellie Jack John's discarded candle is proving to be disturbingly hypnotic for David.

Eventually, David is snatched up in a bright flash of light in front of Keith and disappears. The locals – including David's dad, Dr Wix (David Hargreaves) – put this disappearance down to a devastating lightning accident, but Keith knows that the most obvious answer is no longer the simplest one.

And, as Keith slowly starts to succumb to the power of the candle, the reality facing him begins to become highly distorted as Arthurian legends start manifesting in the real world and Keith faces a real struggle to rescue David.

Behind the Displacement

Earthfasts was a five episode children's drama which went out as part of the Children's BBC schedule in early 1994. Episodes aired on Wednesday afternoons in the 5.10pm slot on BBC1 before being repeated the following Sunday on BBC2 in a mid-morning slot. A solitary series repeat aired in July 1996.

The five episodes which comprised the serial's run originated in the pages of the 1966 *Earthfasts* novel written by William Mayne. And, not content with merely adapting this novel for children's TV, the legendary Marilyn Fox (*Jackanory, Running Scared*) also directed the series.

In conjunction with Fox's wealth of talent, the series was also able to call upon the weighty experience of Ilona Sekacz (*Elidor, Foxtales*) who composed the series' soundtrack and Richard Callanan (*Dark Season, Maid Marian*) in the position of producer.

Recalling the audition and filming process, Chris Downs reflects:

"The BBC contacted one of my teachers and he passed the info on to us saying 'You're welcome to audition for this role' on such and such a date. I had three auditions before I got the part. It was my first TV role and I was thrilled.

Rehearsals took place in London for a week with filming taking place in Richmond, North Yorkshire between August and October 1993. It was a lot to take in but the team made sure everything was taken care of; this helped the other actors and I feel comfy in our roles and we really got along"

Confronting the Stones

Having been hand reared on a diet of dark and disturbing children's TV shows such as *Tom's Midnight Garden* and *Moondial*, it came as no surprise that *Earthfasts* would pique my interest so acutely.

Bristling with unsettling explorations of anguish, loss, time travel and ghostly apparitions, the show felt custom-made to tap into the darker recesses of my curious childhood brain. And, way back as an 11 year old, I couldn't help but succumb to its eerie grandeur with a terror-stricken glee.

All these years later, I was struggling to reorganise the jumbled fragments of *Earthfasts* memories swilling around my brain. Sure, the ominous power was still upfront and proud, but, apart from that, all I could remember was Mad Joe from *EastEnders* and a drummer boy.

Being a rather vague assortment of memories, I decided it was time to cast my forensic eye back over the series. However, could I really expect that disquieting atmosphere of ill ease to *still* infiltrate every square inch of the show's narrative?

Well, with Marilyn Fox on directing duties, it's no surprise that the series delivers in the atmosphere stakes. Using a stripped back, but powerful approach, Fox manages to tease out all the foreboding brilliance of William Mayne's novel with her characteristic efficiency.

With an emphasis on the rolling hills of North Yorkshire – the series was filmed around Richmond – Fox concentrates the colour scheme on that of earthy greens and browns, but also sets many scenes at night to underline *Earthfasts'* clash between the natural world and the unknown.

Being one of the final shows that Fox directed, the series acts as a brilliant example of everything that made her such a crucial part of children's TV history. Downs remembers his time working with Marilyn Fox fondly:

> *"It was excellent! She had a very subtle, warm approach and was full of character. She always provided great advice on my performance, so*

I listened to everything she had to say. We became very close as professional work colleagues and kept in touch for a while after filming"

The atmospheric smarts of the show are given further substance by Ilona Sekazc's score. Calling upon a creepy concoction of horns and woodwind instruments, Sekazc establishes the woozy air of anguish and helplessness pervading the lives of our young protagonists.

And Mayne's characters of Keith and David are an intriguing pair of lads. Okay, they're not wildly different, David is slightly more cavalier and Keith a tad more anxious, but the brand of philosophy they display shows just how insightful children can be.

Nevertheless, Keith and David sometimes exhibit a brand of angst which is a little *too* overpowering. This robs the characters of any sense of humour – so beloved of teenagers and perfectly captured in Russell T Davies' *Dark Season* – but it's a small criticism to level at *Earthfasts*, especially when the young cast deliver with real style.

With regional accents as rich and thick as the finest gravy to cover a Yorkshire pudding, Chris Downs and Paul Nicholls help to ingrain the serial with an authentic and gritty charm. Meanwhile, it's fascinating to see Bryan Dick, so early into his successful career, delivering the goods. Downs has good memories of working with his young co-stars:

"We were friendly, professional and considerate to each other, because that helps you works under pressure. We had a good relationship as we'd spent so much time in each other's company; staying in so many hotels in London and Yorkshire really brought us together.

If you could see the outtakes reel then you'd understand just how well we gelled. There was a huge buzz on set and it was really rewarding when we did everything right. We had a right laugh together once everything was done and dusted"

Paul Nicholls maintained a regular presence on British TV following the series, so his talents speak for themselves. Chris Downs, sadly, did not pursue a career in TV despite his natural aptness for acting. Discussing how acting never quite worked out for him, Downs explains:

"My Mum and Dad got divorced shortly after I finished filming Earthfasts. I had to move and my Dad emigrated to Ireland. I was so busy with exams, school productions and working behind a local bar that it was difficult fitting in auditions from my casting agency.

Sadly, I never really got another shot at a decent role or any recalls; I only had about four auditions in three years. I wanted to pursue my dream of becoming an actor and director, but it would have involved paying huge fees and moving down to London which wasn't really an option at the time"

Despite the groggy air permeating the characters' lives, the pace of *Earthfasts* is far from sluggish. In fact, if anything it's *too* generous with its pace.

The first episode, for example, starts with Keith and David investigating the standing stones and, moments later, Nellie Jack John emerges from the hillside. It feels like half an episode has already passed, but it's actually only a few minutes. It makes for a bewildering start and I couldn't help but think that perhaps the series would have benefitted from an extra episode.

Earthfasts certainly needs a little bit more room to breathe, but this doesn't stop the story's framework from containing an intriguing set of themes. Children stave off the insanity of life by assuring themselves that everything they hold dear will be eternal. Deep down, of course, they know that everything could be taken away and they may find themselves stranded from any normality.

And that's why Nellie Jack John's shift in realities is such a powerful demonstration of the risks the world poses. Nellie Jack John no longer has any control over his own life and appears destined to be lost forever, so it's not surprising that David's disappearance affects Keith so dramatically.

There's a telling scene of significance where a distraught Keith is trudging through the streets deep in thought whilst gleeful, innocent children run past him. It's a subtle nod at the problems adulthood will bring as the lack of responsibility granted by childhood gradually slips away.

Although the rigors of the adult world may seem stressful to Keith and David, there are hints peppered throughout *Earthfasts* that, even though adulthood looks perplexing, it's an arena not to be feared.

The locals' gracious acceptance of a boggart causing mischief indicates that the true nature of the world is something you grow into gradually. And it's a comforting revelation for Keith and David, particularly when they have to deal with giant stone men marching across the moors with a penchant for stealing pigs.

It's intriguing to investigate these themes, but the plot can feel a little muddled and perplexing at times. It's not helped by the breakneck speed at which it unfolds and the myriad themes vying for my attention certainly left me baffled at times.

Nevertheless, due to the unsettling brand of unease that the serial delivers, it's retains the ability to engender a real determination for the viewer to uncover all the answers. And, credit to Marilyn Fox, it comes together neatly in the end with all the characters finding closure.

Forgotten Great?

Granted, it's not *quite* perfect, but *Earthfasts* is still a worthy addition to that long line of chilling children's TV shows. Disturbingly claustrophobic, the show has a compelling plot which, assuming you overlook its occasional weaknesses, delivers a heavy dose of anxiety for our young protagonists and forces them to confront some challenging themes.

The crowning achievement of *Earthfasts* is its wonderful production on what could have been a very testing adaptation. With Marilyn Fox involved, it's a little foolish to contemplate that this could ever have been an issue and, as expected, she stamps her usual seal of quality on it.

CLAPPERBOARD

ITV
1972 - 1982

Whilst television is certainly an integral part of childhood entertainment (and anyone who says otherwise is a crashing bore), cinema offers an equally entertaining route of escapism for the imagination to hurtle down.

And, with a trip to the cinema, you're guaranteed huge visuals, special effects and acting from some of the biggest, most talented actors in the world – although I still stand by my belief that Gwyneth Powell's turn as Mrs McClusky in *Grange Hill* was a definitive masterclass in acting.

Everyone remembers their first trip to the cinema and, for most (unless they're a crashing bore), it remains a lifelong obsession. Sure, the quality of popcorn available in the foyer is diametrically opposed to the advances in cinema technology, but that rush of excitement as the lights go down never diminishes.

Cinema is a fine and admirable obsession, but it's not really got anything to do with the main thrust of this book, has it? Well, actually, one of the finest children's TV shows ever produced was all about the world of cinema, so let's take a look at the sharp clap of *Clapperboard*.

Lights! Camera! Action!

Hosted by Chris Kelly, *Clapperboard* is a comprehensive look at the entire length and breadth of cinema. Very much an arts documentary series, *Clapperboard* investigates not only the contemporary world of cinema, but also its rich history. And, to ensure that no stone is left unturned, almost every conceivable aspect of film is put under the microscope to analyse how all that celluloid magic ends up on the big screen.

Investigating up and coming films, Chris Kelly can, one episode, find himself nestling up with Roger Moore on the set of The Spy Who Loved Me, whilst another episode may find him taking a behind the scenes look at the production of Bugsy Malone.

When it comes to investigating the vast history of cinema, Kelly is keen to delve into the world of Western film heroes, early Hollywood musicals and certain episodes are reserved for exclusive tributes to stars such as Charlie Chaplin and Arthur Askey.

And, with a passionate interest in the minutiae of film making, *Clapperboard* also finds time to dedicate episodes to the Elstree carpentry shop and film cameraman Oswald Morris.

Notes from the Production Office

Over a period of 10 years, Granada Television produced 483 episodes of *Clapperboard*, with episodes appearing late in the afternoon slot reserved for children's television on ITV. The series was produced by Muriel Young (who presented the occasional episode when Chris Kelly was unavailable) and film historian Graham Murray who wrote and compiled the episodes.

Despite Granada having a very good reputation for retaining their material (virtually nothing of note is missing from the mammoth *Coronation Street* archives), *Clapperboard* didn't fare so well with close to 300 episodes missing.

Another Granada series which suffered from the woes of televisual wiping was *Cinema*; fronted by Leslie Halliwell it was an evening documentary series which focused on the world of cinema and would prove to be the inspiration for *Clapperboard*.

Following the dissolution of London's ITV contractor Associated-Rediffusion in 1968, Muriel Young found herself heading north to Granada where she ended up in charge of children's programming and, inspired by *Cinema*, she set about creating something similar, but for a younger audience and, so indebted to *Cinema* it was, the pilot episode was titled *Junior Cinema*.

Leslie Halliwell and Graham Murray (who had also worked on *Cinema)* were brought into devise the initial construct of the series and set up the pilot episode. Chris Kelly was in place for the pilot episode having been recommended by Muriel Young who had worked with him on *Junior Criss Cross Quiz*.

Leslie Halliwell soon drifted away from the production due to his various duties as chief film buyer for ITV, but he appeared in the very first episode 'Illusions' with Chris Kelly and made sporadic appearances afterwards. The eventual title of the series proper ended up as *Clapperboard* after ITV's head of programmes picked the name from a list of suggestions drawn up by Graham Murray.

Trip to the Cinema

The closing credits of the last ever *Clapperboard* episode aired a few months before I was born, so, in this post-*Clapperboard* world – and hamstrung by a lack of repeats and Granada's wiping policy – there was very little chance of me ever making an acquaintance out of the show.

However, British television is a robust entity and, thanks to the infancy of home taping, many episodes have survived. Whilst the majority of these lie in various, inaccessible (but safe) archives, several episodes have ended up in private hands and, eventually, online for curious eyes.

I went into Clapperboard with very little background knowledge of the show, but by the end of watching the episodes, I was absolutely blown away by the sheer dedication to its subject and the series' meticulous approach.

Most striking was the balance that the series kept between intellectual content and the attention span of youngsters – although Chris Kelly once remarked that the audience was aged from seven to seventy.

The terms highbrow and children's TV are rarely seen in the same sentence, but in *Clapperboard* they're entwined constantly. No aspect feels too childish or reductive, but neither does it become a weighty exhibition of intellectual exclusivity. And talking of Chris Kelly, he sums up the Clapperboard ethos to a tee.

Preceded, initially, by an opening theme tune which sounds suspiciously like Supercalifragilisticexpialidocious and, later, a much more modern theme tune drenched in 70s funk and Moog synthesisers, Chris Kelly hosts the show in a seemingly never ending array of blazer jackets which take in the whole gamut of 70s colour schemes.

Educated at Cambridge, Kelly's learned vowels stamp an intellectual authority onto *Clapperboard* from the very start which is in keeping with the highbrow intentions of the series. Kelly is no droning bore, though, and his presenting instinct shines as he demonstrates a charming enthusiasm for the many subjects served up.

Rather than going for a magazine style format, the series focuses each episode on a particular subject. And the aim of these chosen subjects is twofold: firstly, they tap into contemporary cinema matters and, secondly, they provide an educational background for the first point e.g. if Michael Caine has a new film out, there could be a two part special on his career to help fuel the viewer's interest in Maurice Micklethwaite.

It's a worthy approach to engaging the viewer and accounts for the enrapturing effect of the series; it barely diverts from this path and helps to engender a sense of reliability every time you hear those Moogs kick in.

The vast range of topics on offer are what truly defines the wonder of *Clapperboard*. It's an exhaustive run through the entire scope of cinema and delivers a highly professional slice of television. Sure, episodes such as 'Films Starring Horses' may sound incredibly niche, but it's a worthy look at a rarely explored avenue of film.

Likewise, the thought of spending two episodes at Samuelson Film Service may not sound thrilling, but it's actually a fascinating examination of the support behind filmmakers. These episodes may sound serious, and they are to some extent, but they never slide into tedious academia thanks to the compelling analyses on offer.

The most immediate interest comes from the episodes that take us behind the scenes of up and coming films. Airing in an age where DVD extras and Wikipedia articles were nothing short of unimaginable, *Clapperboard* provides the perfect dose of trivia to keep the curiosity of young film buffs sated.

Okay, it removes that little bit of magic from the finished product when you see that Roger Moore doesn't do his own stunts and that C3PO is actually Anthony Daniels in a suit, but the detailed interviews conducted are another example of how much *Clapperboard* respects its young audience.

Chris Kelly *could* ask Julian Glover whether he gets to play with any of Bond's gadgets, but instead he asks pressing questions such as the differences between directions on a Bond film and those in a Royal Shakespeare Company production. He also avoids spending too much time discussing the Green Cross Code man with Dave Prowse and instead cuts in with the somewhat awkward question of how he feels that Darth Vader is redubbed over his dulcet Somerset tones.

It's a manner which sums up the determination of *Clapperboard* to provide a detailed study of the medium and has rarely been matched since.

A Hit with the Critics?

A stunning and quite remarkable take on documentaries for children, *Clapperboard* thrives on its refusal to serve up a reductive look at cinema. Instead, the passion of the team behind the programme allows them to invest their efforts into highly detailed studies of the many components involved in making a film.

And, after watching it, regardless of your age, you'll appreciate the world of films like never before.

BREAK IN THE SUN

BBC1
1981

Our teenage years can be a bit of a nightmare what with having to worry about acne, how cool our trainers are and, most importantly, the opposite sex. However, these are all rather superficial worries and, in the grand scheme of things, they're the least contributing factors towards teenage angst.

For some teenagers, the very real rigours of life can soon come calling and completely deconstruct everything they've held dear and believed would be eternal. And, when this type of upheaval comes to town, you need take a *Break in the Sun*.

Getting Away From it All

Trapped within an abusive environment, Patsy Bligh (Nicola Cowper) is a young girl whose spirit is slowly being dismantled. There's a need to escape from this soul destroying landscape, but where can she go? She's just a child and has none of the resources required to break free.

Plucked from the secure warmth of her Margate home – where the grandmotherly Mrs Broadley (Kathleen Heath) doted upon her – Patsy is now trapped in Deptford thanks to her mother, Sylvia Green (Catherine Chase), getting married and having a baby with Eddie Green (Brian Hall).

Now, the main thrust of Patsy's woes and worries come directly from the embittered rage of Eddie who belittles her verbally and gets handy with his fists. It's an exercise in anxiety which is so distressing that her nights have become a real horrorshow of bedwetting.

Obviously, Patsy is shaken up and feels completely alienated as her mother is far too busy with the new baby. Sure, Patsy's got her mate Kenny Granger (Kevin Taffurelli) - ginger, portly and prone to swimming in the murky Thames - but there's only so much support his bespectacled form can offer.

The only way that Patsy feels able to escape all this hideousness appears to be by immersing herself in the world of drama. She's a bit of a starlet next to her monotone peers and, just maybe, this precocious talent is going to help her escape the doldrums of Deptford.

One day, Patsy spies a curious old boat down at the quay which houses an acting troupe who are travelling up and down the coast performing a production of 'A Happy Release'. And they're heading towards Margate where the comforting bosom of Mrs Broadley resides.

Patsy, of course, soon finds her eyes twinkling with visions of treading the boards and finding refuge from the bothersome Eddie. And, by a stroke of luck, half term's coming up, so wouldn't it be just spiffing for her to join the production and sail all her worries away?

Unlike Eddie, the actors are fully functioning grownups with well calibrated moral compasses, so they exhibit a real sense of concern. After all, they're not keen on whisking her away from her parents into a world of seafaring performance. At least, not without her parents' permission.

Determined to get away from it all, Patsy tricks Eddie into writing some vague nonsense allowing her to go on a school trip. The actors are overjoyed and take her on board before heading off onto the high seas for deepest Kent.

Patsy, of course, has already skipped school by this point, so a teacher heads round to see her parents and find out what's going on. Once this revelation of playing hooky becomes apparent, all hell breaks loose and Patsy's distraught mother finally starts laying down the law at Eddie's door.

Kenny, after being harassed by his saccharine, but well-meaning mother (Patsy Rowlands), reveals that he saw Patsy getting on a boat. Eddie's bundled out of the house and told to find out where she's got to and his detective work reveals that the boat's headed for Kent.

Perhaps driven by a glimmer of guilt, Eddie doesn't see any point in getting the police involved, so he teams up with Kenny in order to bring Patsy home safely.

Packing the Cases

Break in the Sun started off life as a 1980 novel by the esteemed children's author Bernard Ashley. Keen to tell stories based upon his environment – namely life in East London – *Break in the Sun* was inspired by a visit to Drew School in Silvertown where he noticed a rather melancholy girl surveying the Thames.

Wondering what this girl was thinking and imagining the world she inhabited, Ashley set to work crafting a novel which he felt would echo her bleak existence, but also underline her fighting spirit. The novel was well received and Alan England was soon adapting the novel for the BBC.

Six episodes of *Break in the Sun* aired in the early months of 1981 in the 5.05pm slot reserved for older viewers, a single repeat airing came during spring 1982. Getting comfy in the director's chair was Roger Singleton-Turner who would later direct *Grange Hill* and *The Demon Headmaster*.

Oh What a Lovely Break!

Being a big fan of Bernard Ashley's writing talents in print and on television, *Break in the Sun* offered the tantalising prospect of delving into Ashley's trademark tone of grit and brutal honesty shone through a prism of relatable characters.

And, although it's an adaptation, Alan England has managed to communicate all those nuances of teen alienation and the crushing angst Ashley infused his original text with. Most importantly, that recurring Ashley motif of running away is pumping strongly through the veins of Patsy.

Taking a closer look at Patsy reveals that she's a curious character; with alternating layers of aspirations and anxiety, there's an intriguing cacophony of turmoil going on within her young mind and it's well played by Nicola Cowper.

Despite Cowper's burgeoning skills, the true star of the piece is Eddie or, as he's perhaps best known 'Terry the chef' from *Fawlty Towers*. Appearing, at first, to be nothing more than a boorish Cockney thug, as *Break in the Sun* unfurls, we discover that Eddie has many coatings which are gradually stripped away. And it's once Eddie teams up with Kenny that this transformation begins to take place.

Now, Kenny and Eddie are like chalk and cheese, but it's this contrast in personality which sparks off a change in emotional output for Eddie. In between despairing about Kenny's obesity, he takes on a paternal role and begins to share insights into the rigours of growing up in his father's shadow.

And it's Kenny who finally opens Eddie's eyes to the

gruesome truth that he's to blame for all of Patsy's misdemeanours. It's a complex piece of drama to be aiming at children, but the series pulls it off maturely and never sinks into the realms of soppy atonement.

It's this frankness which informs every aspect of *Break in the Sun* and an approach which was brave and unique in the early 80s. Okay, *Grange Hill* had been exploring mature themes for a few years, but never focusing on so few characters and with such brutal, unflinching honesty.

Break in the Sun pulls no punches in taking on themes such as death, anxiety, suicide and, finally, redemption; it's all done without the comedy antics of Tucker Jenkins et al, so *Break in the Sun* is clearly cut from a different cloth. How, though, does the series pan out?

Well, early on, I began to fear that Eddie and Kenny's pursuit – where they constantly seem to be one Kentish town behind Patsy – would become a tiresome slog, but as Eddie's whole id is slowly dissected and reassessed you can't help but be sucked into the narrative.

Patsy's journey, too, takes on some important themes for children to observe and understand such as child abuse and alienation. Deeper still, there's a clear message that running away can be like so many other childhood endeavours: impulsive and ill-conceived.

Even if she had managed to reunite with Mrs Broadley, it would have only acted as the briefest of respites for Patsy before she was shipped back to Deptford. Running away from her problems is clearly not the answer and, as she eventually discovers, Patsy needs to literally face them head on.

And, whilst Eddie clearly has his road to Damascus

moment, Patsy faces the incredibly difficult task of having to trust Eddie. The series ends with Patsy edging tentatively towards Eddie and indicates that she's capable of acknowledging change and trading it for hope.

Fun in the Sun?

With a tone that feels more like a Mike Leigh kitchen sink drama and the incredibly detailed character of Eddie, *Break in the Sun* is a remarkable piece of television. And the way in which it confronts its uncomfortable themes is done with such maturity that it's easy to forget you're watching children's TV.

But you *are* watching children's TV and this is what makes *Break in the Sun* so impressive. Coupled with the relatable plight of Patsy and the examination of childhood alienation, it's a realistic series which can't fail to succeed in captivating the audience.

It does this with an ease that allows the series to go beyond the realms of *just* being a children's TV show as, following an online piece I wrote on the series, many people got in touch to reveal that *Break in the Sun* had given them the courage to stand up to child abuse. And, to induce that type of positive reaction, there's surely no stronger evidence for the power of TV.

HOKEY COKEY

BBC1
1983, 1985

There's nothing like having a good old dance and, believe me, after a few barley wines, you just try and keep me away from the dance floor. And, although I may not be the best dancer on the planet, I'm certainly better than any three year old.

However, children, through no fault of their own, are still struggling with co-ordinated movements at the age of three, so it's understandable that they can't 'Vogue' let alone dance like Rudolf Nureyev. But how do they get started on the path towards honing their fleet footed Macarena skills?

Well, it all starts with the hokey cokey song which is just perfect for their restless, wriggling limbs. First off, it's ridiculously easy for a three year old to put their left leg in and then their right leg out and, secondly, it's gleefully fun to shake it all about whilst screaming such simple, catchy lyrics.

More importantly, it gives children a bit more confidence in moving around and engaging with the world around them. This advice, of course, isn't just limited to a bit of participatory dance; it's also served up in the televisual equivalent which is named, not surprisingly, *Hokey Cokey*.

Hokey and Indeed Cokey

Helmed by Don (Don Spencer) who is aided and abetted by either Chloe (Chloe Ashcroft) or Carol (Carol Chell), *Hokey Cokey* is a children's show with plenty of tricks up its sleeve. Each episode holds up a particular concept to the spotlight for Don and Co to scrutinise and help the viewers understand how this crazy old world works. Choice notions considered ripe for exploration include jungle animals, the night sky, machinery and even good old fashioned jumping.

And how are themes explored? Well, it's more a case of how *aren't* these themes explored?

Don is never too far from a guitar, so, through the medium of song, he's able to belt out oddball classics such as "Old Woman Tossed up in a Basket", Chloe, meanwhile, is also prone to dusting down her vocal cords to serenade the listeners alongside her interpretive dance skills.

Storytelling is integral to the show and the presenters frequently regale viewers with tales of 'Meg and Mog' and 'Victoria Kangaroo' to help calm things down for a few moments before launching into more active explorations of the episode's theme.

Taking the young viewer by the hand, the presenters get up to all sorts such as Carol Chell flicking paper boats around water, Don Spencer playing games of skill and Chloe Ashcroft discovering which objects sink and which ones float.

All this action is solely contained within the constraints of the studio, but stock footage is also used to provide a grander sense of the themes being proffered such as kangaroos sweeping across the Australian desert or just a load of children losing their minds over a giant inflatable.

In amongst these many methods of feeding crucial life lessons into young brains, there's also time to squeeze in two clown puppets named Hokey and Cokey. These merrymakers join in with the fun by singing, dancing and even examining the intricacies of the Highway Code.

Episodes end with a brief prompt from one of the presenters to stick an ever changing limb either in and out to kickstart the closing credits where children dance wildly.

Planning the Dance

Hokey Cokey aired in the See-Saw slot on BBC1 and provided 26 episodes of lunchtime viewing for children which spanned two series between 1983 and 1985. Episodes continued to be repeated on BBC1 and BBC2 up until 1989.

Christine Hewitt produced the series and had previously worked on children's TV shows such as *Play School*, *It's Monday* and *Stop Go*. The *Play School* connection was further strengthened by the presence of the legendary Cynthia Felgate as executive producer. And, yes, that's right, Don Spencer, Carol Chell and Chloe Ashchroft had all chalked up lengthy stints on *Playschool*.

Putting it In and Out

Did I remember *Hokey Cokey?* Well, yes, I most certainly did, having watched countless editions as a young lad. Frustratingly, I couldn't remember anything apart from the show's title, so it was most certainly worth an investigation.

As the opening credits of children dancing the hokey cokey, unfolded in front of me, and the manic child led rendition of the accompanying song blared out, I suddenly had that pang of nostalgic yearning for my front room in those fuzzy childhood afternoons.

Conceived from the same DNA as *Play School*, it's not a startling revelation that *Hokey Cokey* is somewhat derivative of

Big Ted et al, but *Play School* was such a fine example of children's TV that it's a fine blueprint to draw from.

Key to *Hokey Cokey's* success is its ever shifting features; one moment we're indulging in the musical nonsense of the 'Hooray for Eyes' song, the next we're hotfooting towards the adventures of Meg and Mog in space before conking out in front of a swift puppet show from Hokey and Cokey.

And it's this quick, veering nature which prevents boredom from ever digging its claws deep into your brain; if something in the show bores you then don't worry, something right up your alley will be along in a minute such as Don getting to grips with a pneumatic drill or impersonating a hippo.

The frenetic brilliance of this content is matched by the equally superb presenting work by the proprietors of *Hokey Cokey's* universe. No doubt helped by the *Play School* bonds giving them a mutual understanding, there's an excellent synergy between the presenters.

Brimming with antipodean charm, Don Spencer is on impressive form with a hearty masculine confidence. Always ready to showcase his guitar playing, Don is an immense entertainer with the skills to present, sing and act, so it's difficult to shift your gaze from his eclectic talents.

Chloe Ashcroft is just fantastic in her array of 1980s jumpsuits and flowing blouses, but her magnificence isn't just limited to her fashion sense. Blessed with a perfectly pitched singing voice, she also exudes a wide eyed, barmy brilliance to pique the attention of pre-schoolers.

Just a smidgeon more grounded is Carol Chell, but believe me, she still finds time for pulling plenty of faces and making noises as she splashes around with water. She's brimming over with a kind, welcoming charm and comes across as the greatest primary school teacher you never had.

Shake It All About?

Although there's nothing in *Hokey Cokey* which *quite* matches the iconic status of Big Ted, Hamble and going "through the window" from *Play School*, it's fair to say that *Hokey Cokey* is a fine relative of the legendary, long running *Play School*.

Thanks to the great chemistry bubbling away between its cast and crew, *Hokey Cokey* delivers a regular dose of measured brilliance. Sure, it's off its rocker and completely barmy at times, but what a perfect analogy for the world that the young viewers are growing up in.

TALES FROM FAT TULIP'S GARDEN

ITV
1985, 1987

The world can be a beguiling and confounding place at the best of times for adults, therefore, for young children, it's an incredibly baffling place at *all* times. And there are so many intricacies to the way the world works that it's no surprise children turn to their imagination to fill in the blanks.

Take a look out the window, for example, what's that robin doing hopping about in the garden? Well, he's probably just scrabbling around in the dirt looking for worms. However, to a three year old, Mr Robin could very well be on a treasure hunt for gold and jewels in the dirt.

Despite the child's interpretation of the events being completely nonsensical, it demonstrates how the power of imagination is an early building block in the world of storytelling. Without these early forays into creativity there simply wouldn't be any narrative quality in our entertainment.

And to help remind youngsters of the importance of cultivating their inventiveness – and the fantastic results that can be achieved – is *Tales from Fat Tulip's Garden*.

Garden Tales

Fat Tulip isn't the sharpest tack in the box and he's certainly not prone to making good decisions, but his heart is in the right place and he definitely knows where his stomach is. In fact, his portly frame is no surprise when his favourite sandwich contains chocolate spread, peanut butter, jam, cold potato and a fried egg.

Taking up the position of Fat Tulip's best friend – and with a body shape in sharp contrast – is Thin Tim. Now, whilst Thin Tim is merely an eccentric chap keen on sleeping in the airing cupboard, Fred the Baddy is an altogether different proposition in the friends stakes for Fat Tulip.

Prone to communicating through the medium of old kippers and stink bombs, Fred the Baddy is a purple bodied, criminal imp who considers Fat Tulip to be his best friend; an outlook which is not entirely shared by Fat Tulip.

Thankfully, the law is on hand to curtail Fred the Baddy's activities and generally poke its nose into Fat Tulip's business in the form of Inspector Challiner. Sadly, this particular policeman is as equally dim-witted as Fat Tulip, yet shot through with a hefty dose of arrogant confidence.

At the same time these humans are busy interacting with tins of paint, lost keys and jam doughnuts, there's a whole world going on beneath their feet. And the busy animal kingdom living in Fat Tulip's garden is equally prone to madcap adventures.

Ernie and Sylv are the resident pond dwelling frogs who live a fairly placid life in the mud and water until the arrival of the 'stinkers' Peter, Paul and Mary who are a bunch of filthy toads hell bent on destroying the wild beauty of Fat Tulip's garden.

Also causing havoc amongst the blades of grass is Dorian the dog, an ex-police dog more suited to sniffing out jam doughnuts than burglars. And Lewis Collins is the deluded tortoise who believes he can leap over Fat Tulip's house and is also a master of disguise (particularly as a fruitcake).

There's a real gaggle of characters making up the dynamics

of *Tales from Fat Tulip's Garden*, but rather than containing a cast of thousands, they're all conveyed through the expressions, sounds and visuals of Tony Robinson as he dashes and leaps manically round the house, garden and woods.

Tending the Garden

Comprising 13 episodes, *Tales from Fat Tulip's Garden* was a 1985 Central Independent Television program produced by ITV which aired at 12pm and, on the same day, at 4pm. The series was repeated once in 1986. A follow up series – *Fat Tulip Too* - followed in 1987 for 13 episodes.

A collaboration between drama school buddies Tony Robinson and Debbie Gates, *Tales From Fat Tulip's Garden* originated in a series of stories created by Debbie's young daughter; they centred around the adventures of a boy called Henry and a rotund tulip called Fat Tulip.

Robinson was smitten with the idea of a character called Fat Tulip and, with his creative juices flowing, soon conceived several other characters. And, keen to promote the sense of imagination, Robinson decided to play all the characters, allowing viewers to interpret them in their mind's eye.

Gates wanted Robinson to inject something from his own childhood into the series, so a house that he had played in as a child – Little Monkhams in Woodford – was chosen and the homeowners were advised to not clean it in order to preserve the cobwebby look.

Unfortunately, Little Monkhams was destroyed in a suspicious fire in 2007, so only the gutted remains now stand.

Still surviving, thankfully, is Knighton Wood – part of Epping Forest – which is opposite Little Monkhams and features heavily in several episodes.

Kevin Stoney produced the music for the series and remembers his involvement fondly:

"Debbie Gates, the producer and creator of Fat Tulip's Garden, was passionate about producing imaginative programmes for children's television in a storytelling format. So with co-writer Tony Robinson, the concept of Fat Tulip's Garden was born.

Debbie, and director Jeremy McCracken, wanted the music and graphics to reflect an edge to the series, so I created many squelchy and unusual sampling effects. These ended up in the main theme music and were also used for various character stings.

Because you never visually saw the characters in each story, Tony (the narrator) had to describe and act out each character to camera. The musical stings for each character also played an important part to conjure up an image in the imaginations of the children watching it.

I remember having great fun working with the production team. It was a marvellously creative time! I fondly remember the post-production team – with film editor Peter Spenceley – being in stitches when I took in my strange musical compositions to represent each of Fat Tulip's characters!

I continued working with Debbie Gates when she went on to produce the next series - Fat Tulip Too. She also produced and co-wrote Revolting Animals, Jellyneck, and Gumtree - all with the same unique storytelling concept and quirky music by myself"

Two books were published by Hippo Books in 1985 to promote the series – 'Tales from Fat Tulip's Garden' and 'Meet a Dog Called Dorian' – which gave author credits for

Debbie Gates and Tony Robinson with the illustrations provided by Heather Munro.

Imaginative Storytelling

Back in the mid-1980s I led a charmed existence and this was mostly due to the fact that I was too young to go to either school or work. Luckily, I was certainly old enough to watch the TV. And that's how, one lazy afternoon, I found myself round at my cousin's house watching *Tales from Fat Tulip's Garden*.

Despite the house being full of adults and other manic children, the show had me so transfixed with Robinson's madcap antics that it felt as though everything around me had stopped as I stepped into another world formed on the backbone of my creativity.

Unfortunately, the name of the series made less of an impact on my rapidly developing memory, so for many years I was only able to describe it as being "that show with Tony Robinson telling all them stories in a house" – a description which failed to spark any hint of recall from my peers.

Then, with the advent of the internet, I finally had the means to track down the name of the series. And, in a rare twist of fortune, *Tales from Fat Tulip's Garden* was one of those curiously forgotten TV shows blessed with a DVD release, so I was well poised to re-analyse the series.

Having been 30 years since I last imagined Fat Tulip's portly, bespectacled frame, would it still run riot through my imagination? After all, my creative capabilities had been subjected to vast flights of fancy in the intervening years, particularly as a frustrated teenage boy.

Thankfully, these fears were allayed from the moment Robinson bounded on screen. Such is his dedication to the series – every facet of it pumps frenetically round his every artery – that he quite literally becomes *Tales from Fat Tulip's Garden*.

With an ability to pluck so many characters from the creative soup swilling around in his brainbox, Robinson manages to create a seamless dialogue which is bordering on schizophrenic. Far removed from the terrors of mental illness, though, this is actually amazing improvisation.

Setting down markers for the general narrative, Robinson gleefully leaps and gurns through a surreal set of plot beats to foster an exciting set of stories where the conclusion is almost impossible to predict.

Its anarchic outlook on storytelling is a world away from the comfortable, staid performances usually housed in a comfy chair within *Jackanory*. And whilst I'm not averse to a helping of *Jackanory* – or a comfy chair – it's certainly more fun to spend time with its older, punk rock cousin.

And by conjuring up stories which take in mud, slime, filthy toads and tearaway dogs, *Tales from Fat Tulip's Garden* taps into that wonder of all things messy and disgusting that children have a natural affinity with.

Although this creates a foothold into a child's delicate thinking, it's the series' minimalist approach which is its stroke of genius. With just Robinson's interpretations to hand, the viewer has to fill in the visual gaps and create a whole new universe. It's a fine education in understanding the basics of storytelling and how you can take a story in any direction without having to stick to any structural boundaries.

The final jewel in the crown of all this storytelling is the beautiful and idyllic setting of Little Monkhams. The epitome of quirky British charm, it endows *Tales from Fat Tulip's Garden* with a timeless sense of wonder which perfectly complements Fat Tulip's world.

In fact, it's a real shame that *Fat Tulip Too* moved the majority of its filming away from Little Monkhams and out into the big bad world of reality. Somehow it just doesn't feel quite as magical in amongst the verruca socks of Leyton swimming baths and Robinson has stated that, with hindsight, he shouldn't have taken it on the road.

Nonetheless, the charming and quirky tales remain mostly undiminished even if the viewer's attention is distracted by the new perception of scale. And, besides, the action returned purely to Little Monkhams for the final Christmas episode to capture that old magic one last time.

Revisiting Fat Tulip's...

Thanks to my exploits in the world of the lesser known gems of TV, I was invited to contribute towards a 2016 documentary entitled *Imaginative Storytelling Experiences* (www.isedoc.net) which examined the influence of *Tales from Fat Tulip's Garden* on its viewers' imagination and creative abilities.

Filming took place in Knighton Wood down by the very pond that had once been Ernie and Sylv's mud filled home. Oh and Tony Robinson turned up to regale us with his crystal clear memories. Yes, that's right, Sir Tony Robinson, Mr Fat Tulip himself.

And he's a magnificent man, a true cornucopia of energy, articulation and laughter, so meeting him in the flesh was a remarkable experience and one that the three year old version of me — eagerly perched in front of the TV at my cousin's house — would have lost their tiny little mind over.

Following the filming, I went to visit the remains of Little Monkhams which was a short hop, skip and a jump away from Knighton Wood, but the gutted, overgrown remains which greeted me were a sad epitaph for the legacy of *Tales from Fat Tulip's Garden*.

With the jungle of thorns blocking my way at every turn, it felt like the vibrant nature which had once defined the garden was trying to reclaim Little Monkhams and protect it from the rigors of the modern world and unscrupulous property developers.

A little disappointed at seeing a bastion of my childhood reduced to such a dilapidated state, I trudged back through Knighton Wood where, suddenly, I was confronted by a shabby looking fox. Instantly, images began to flood my mind and a story began to form.

Maybe this fox was heading off to raid Inspector Challinor's chicken coop to secure himself a tasty Sunday lunch, but, uh oh, it was the same day that Fat Tulip and Thin Tim were attending a fancy dress party at Inspector Challinor's house dressed as, yep, chickens.

And, with a sudden spring in my step, I realised that the magic of *Fat Tulip's* was still alive and well.

CHOCK-A-BLOCK

BBC1
1981

It wasn't long ago that computers were considered to be nothing more than a bit of sci-fi whimsy. After all, you were guaranteed to see one in *Doctor Who* every week, but getting to see a computer in the flesh was the preserve of a select few.

Come the 1980s, the computer began its lofty rise into a world conquering device which means that, in the modern age, it's a forlorn wrist, pocket or desktop which doesn't contain some form of computer. And television was keen to get on board with this burgeoning industry.

In particular, the BBC initiated their Computer Literacy Project to help Britain get to grips with this new-fangled technology. Shows such as *The Computer Programme* and *Micro Live* were fantastic entry points for adults, but learning about spreadsheets was rather dull for any children watching.

However, just predating the Computer Literacy Project was a show for children with a super computer at the heart of the action. And, although it wouldn't be teaching the rudimental basics of computer programming, there would be plenty of learning in *Chock-a-Block*.

Silicon Sentience

Central to *Chock-a-Block* is the huge yellow mainframe known as Chock-a-Block that has a penchant for digesting blocks and dispensing knowledge through its array of monitors. And it's even vaguely humanised with its crude representation of a face made up of tape reels and flashing lights.

Despite this stab at humanising Chock-a-Block, there's still a need for real life humans to help operate Chock-a-Block and coax out the learning that lurks inside its guts; arriving on an electric chockatruck to help, are the Chockagirl (Carol Leader) and Chockabloke (Fred Harris).

Taking turns in presenting episodes of *Chock-a-Block,* the Chockagirl and Chockabloke get episodes started by feeding a block into Chock-a-Block which leads to a series of pictures – with a rhyming theme for the week e.g. cat, hat, rat – being displayed on Chock-a-Block's monitor. This rhyming imagery soon segues into a brief song accompanied by illustrations such as a jaunty ditty about Dame Trott's chat with her cat. Sometimes the Chockapresenter sings this song into Chock-a-Block and the viewer is treated, for no discernible reason, to a vocoder heavy playback.

Occasionally, if Chock-a-Block is in the mood, the Chockapresenter takes the viewer through simple games e.g. a memory game which involves recalling pairs of rhyming images. Following these frolics, the show's attention shifts to the rockablock. Again, the rhyming element of *Chock-a-Block* is brought to the fore as the Chockapresenter spins the rockablock's reels to match up similar sounding images such as log and dog. A number of these rhyming examples are used to hammer home the rhyming sounds before moving on to another song.

Integrating illustrations and puppets, the Chockapresenter proceeds to sing over – or appear in – a short vignette played out on Chock-a-Block's monitor. These closing sections include Joe Crow flying over a pastoral landscape and Old

King Cole struggling to deal with an industrious mole in his lawn.

And with the completion of this tale, the Chockapresenter ejects the themed block from Chock-a-Block, bids farewell to the viewer and hops onto the chockatruck before hightailing it out of there for another week.

Firing up the Mainframe

Created by the legendary children's TV supremo Michael Cole, *Chock-a-Block* ran for a 13 episode stretch across a single series in 1981; episodes aired on Thursday afternoons in the 1.30pm slot during the early days of legendary lunchtime children's TV slot See-Saw.

Cole was joined by fellow doyen of children's TV production, Nick Wilson, who acted as *Chock-a-Block's* director. Shoring up the striking, visual appeal of *Chock-a-Block* was graphic designer Mina Martinez and designer Mary Penley Edwards with the 'chockatunes' being provided by Peter Gosling.

Chock-a-Block managed to maintain a fairly constant presence on BBC1 and BBC2 throughout the 1980s thanks to repeats, but hasn't been aired since 1989. Sadly, not all of these episodes remain as *Chock-a-Block* fell victim to the BBC's junking policy which continued up until the early 1990s.

Now, it's not *quite* as bad as it sounds as, notwithstanding that six of the original 1" master tapes were junked, the BBC holds off-air recordings of all the episodes. Therefore, the slim chance of a *Chock-a-Block* DVD boxset remains a possibility; just not in its full 1980s broadcast quality.

Operating the System

Chock-a-Block was part of the amazing lineup of lunchtime children's TV that I found myself confronted with as a preschooler, so it was a show firmly ensconced in the seemingly limitless area of my brain known as the nostalgiacampus.

However, it had been 30 or so years since I had last viewed *Chock-a-Block* and my memories were vague to say the least. Luckily, despite no commercial releases being forthcoming, the series was transmitted in an era where home recording was starting to take off.

And, not surprisingly, a number of episodes have found their way online via aging VHS and Betamax tapes, so everything was set for me to revisit *Chock-a-Block* and establish if it was more than "a big yellow computer with some flashy lights and noises" as my memory suggested.

Immediately, *Chock-a-Block* gets you on its side with Peter Gosling's quite phenomenal electropop theme tune. It's a triumphant electro anthem mixing big fat synths with vocoder vocals and sounds like the perfect song for an under-fives night at The Blitz club.

As your sensory receptors are recovering from this aural brilliance, they're immediately shifting into gear as the chockapresenter scoots into town and a series of flashing lights briefly turn the BBC studio into Studio 54. Just as you expect Mick Jagger and Debbie Harry to boogie into shot, the lights come up and you're face to face with Chock-a-Block.

Bright and colourful, the production team have done a great job in replicating a huge computer capable of arresting a child's attention and one which, with all the flashing lights and colours, can also fascinate an adult.

Naturally, a mostly mute and less than sentient computer doesn't have the skills at its disposal to front a TV show on its own, so it's down to the chockapresenters to take charge. And, thanks to their vast experience in children's TV, they take to it like ducks to water.

Fred Harris and Carol Leader had both served time on legendary children's BBC show *Play School*, so it's very much business as usual for them; their bright, friendly personalities prove their worth by helping to draw viewers into this curious world of rhyme, song and story.

Preschool shows are all about learning and the aim of *Chock-a-Block* is to familiarise the viewers with language and all its various flourishes and intricacies. An intention which, on the whole, it achieves. By sugaring the bitter pill of studying with puppets, songs and stories, the chockapresenter is able to sneak in a lesson on linguistics which opens up the possibilities of language.

A disturbingly ugly cat puppet aside, the puppets are cute and welcoming whilst the songs are melodic little earworms – the 'Night and Day' song starts off as an electro-flute tune before morphing into a trancelike mantra straight off of Pink Floyd's 'The Piper at the Gates of Dawn'.

The only section which felt like it was severely chafing my delicate attention span was the rockablock exercise. We've already seen cat rhymed with various words a little too much by this point, so revisiting this apparent 'marvel' of rhyme is akin to Chinese water torture.

Still, repetition is key to learning and, as a thirty-something, I've got very different requirements to a preschooler – although, obviously, both age groups are less than keen on Chinese water torture...

Chock-a-Wonder?

Chock-a-Block certainly spends very little time within the boundaries of reality when it comes to the world of computing, but that's for the adults anyway, so, seriously, who cares?

Computers do, as anyone who's ever picked up a V-Tech knows, help aid learning and *Chock-a-Block* acts as a cheerful conduit to this end. It may not be quite as perfect at Michael Cole's other exploration of linguistics – the amazing *Bric-a-Brac* – but the show's structure is sound enough to let it get away with the odd misjudged folly. A worthy entry into the pantheon of classic children's TV.

THE PIG ATTRACTION

ITV
1993

It's probably clear by now that I've got somewhat of an obsession with retro children's TV, but you may be wondering what kick-started this messy, glorious affair. Well, as the first pangs of adolescence descended upon me, I felt an uncontrollable urge to look back and reminisce over my childhood as it flickered out and hairs began to spring up in the most unmentionable places.

Television, obviously, had been a constant companion throughout childhood, so there was an intense desire to reconnect with what had been shaping my mindset in what felt like a forgotten age. Sure, it only stretched back to a period of 6 – 7 years previous, but to a 10 year old that's almost a lifetime.

As luck would have it, the gods of retro TV were listening and a show which was perfect for my reflective nature was winging its way to me in the form of *The Pig Attraction*.

Welcome, Ladies and Gentlemen! And Swine!

Part documentary, part chat show and part 'show within a show' *The Pig Attraction* is a curious beast which refuses to be defined by a single genre. Hosted by Billie the Pig, *The Pig Attraction's* main focus is committed to delving deep into the world of puppetry and providing an education into what goes on behind the strings.

Helped by puppeteer Simon Buckley, Billie the Pig

interviews stars from the world of puppetry and dissects the various techniques involved in transforming slumped, inanimate puppets into three dimensional beings. Interviews include chats with such puppet luminaries as: Roland Rat, Big Bird, Gerry Anderson, Earl E Bird, Hartley Hare and, uh, Peter Baldwin aka Derek Wilton from *Coronation Street*.

Despite Billie's best efforts to maintain a level of Michael Parkinson slickness, the presence of mischievous puppets backstage means that shows gradually collapse under the weight of intense chaos. In amongst the disorder, a reminder of the *The Pig Attraction's* nostalgic definition is underlined by the helium tones of *Pinky and Perky* singing a pop classic.

Backroom Staff

10 episodes of *The Pig Attraction* aired during mid-1993 in the Children's ITV slot and the series was produced by HTV. Episodes ran to 25 minutes long and were beamed out on Thursdays at 4.15pm. *The Pig Attraction* is an archetypal forgotten show in that it only garnered one series and not a single repeat has aired since.

The series sprouted from an idea put forwards by HTV producer Peter Murphy as Simon Buckley remembers:

"For six years I performed a character on Saturday morning ITV called Nobby the Sheep. Nobby's first show was called Ghost Train and it toured around the country with a different episode each week being produced by a different TV region (we had lots of ITV companies in those days).

In Bristol and Cardiff the shows were produced by HTV and HTV West where Peter Murphy was the producer. Peter had previously worked on 'Rolf's Cartoon Club' which mixed classic cartoons with lessons on animation and wanted to do something similar, but with puppets.

About the same time, having met me through Nobby the Sheep, Peter engaged me to work a puppet pig for an environmental series with Bill Oddie called 'Ask Oddie'. From this, the idea evolved to make the format of the puppet series a chat show with Billie the Pig as its host and with my knowledge and experience at its heart.

It's fair to say that about 90% of the content came from me. I was really keen to use this as a showcase for the vast range of puppetry styles and techniques many of which were not used on television and inspire children with this rich and wonderful art form.

My exact title changed so many times, but basically I basically provided everything from many of the contacts with puppeteers and puppet companies, to an understanding of the subject in hand as well as the set dressing for the puppet workshop and devised the simple 'make and do' elements of the show. I had more pies to have fingers in than I actually had fingers!"

The TV series itself never received a commercial release, but there was merchandise in the form of a CD, tape and vinyl edition of Pinky and Perky's pop renditions which featured throughout the series. Somehow I never got round to purchasing these. Do I feel poorer for missing out? No…

Revisiting our Inspiration

The Pig Attraction was integral in lighting the blue touch paper for my retro TV passion, so I could hardly exclude it from this compendium of curious British children's TV. To do so would be to deny my heritage and a betrayal to that snotty nosed Herbert who, in 1993, was precariously balanced between the sanctity of childhood and the excitement of adolescence.

Hinting at the chaos to come, episodes of *The Pig Attraction* commence with a brief opener where Billie the Pig is struggling to get the show off the ground. Within seconds the production team are papering over the backstage chaos as the energetic theme tune kicks in and Billie bursts onto the glitzy set.

It makes for an impressive opener and, with the lurking sense of pandemonium, suggests an intriguing collision of brilliance and misfortune lies ahead.

The content of *The Pig Attraction* is, undeniably, the brilliance that illuminates the show. This is fuelled by the marvellous character the series has at its disposal in the trotted form of Billie the Pig. I find him an absolutely captivating character, veering wildly from confident media host to panicked porcine as he struggles to keep *The Pig Attraction* together at its thrashing seams.

Puppets, naturally, are rather limited in their movements, so Simon Buckley makes for an essential co-presenter, especially when the intricate movements of the human hand are needed to show how puppets are brought to life. Buckley's enthusiasm for an industry which he has made his home is apparent from the off:

"I was passionate about this show, and the show we started to make was a dream come true for me. It took a few turns that I didn't really like (too many C list puppets plugging their own shows, rather than contributing anything really interesting or funny) and some of the original concept got lost, but even today people thank me for pieces that I filmed

as they provide a really valuable and quite rare record of that kind of puppetry.

I was also thrilled to get such a great series of interviews with Brian Henson, son of Jim, and I am sure that it was my genuine inside knowledge that enabled him to be very open with me and share so much with the audience, beyond what we had been told he would be prepared to do.

Too often when someone interviews a puppeteer they ask the same overly simplistic questions like "do you get the strings tangled?" Yaaaaaaawn! Thankfully the fact that I knew my subject helped to make up for the fact that I really wasn't great on camera... I think I was more wooden than any of the puppets! And, boy, did I wear some shocking clothes!"

The backstage chaos – which gradually spreads to the main set – is a fun diversion from the rather more serious documentary sections. It's a rich source of laughter which allows the puppets to flex their comedy muscles and helps keep the show grounded in the world of children's TV. However, the shadow of *The Muppet Show* hangs heavily over these sections, so, at times, feels a bit too familiar to be truly unique.

For fans of children's TV the biggest thrill comes when *The Pig Attraction* revisits past stars of the puppet world. The most impressive one featured in the series comes when that rodent megastar Roland Rat conducts a poolside interview with Billie about his life and times. These sections feature impressive bursts of knowledge, reflection and personality to a degree where you forget these are just inanimate puppets.

And, of course, *The Pig Attraction,* provides a welcome comeback for Hartley Hare from *Pipkins* as he features in several episodes as part of the backstage antics. Given the dearth of readily available *Pipkins* material at the time, it's a tremendous bonus and one that sums up the special nature of *The Pig Attraction*.

Pork Attraction?

Airing in an age where the internet was the luxury preserve of a privileged few, *The Pig Attraction* was a rare opportunity to broaden my knowledge on the history of British children's TV. It also planted the seeds for my future endeavours in this niche. And niche is a very important word here.

You see, although I adored *The Pig Attraction* when it aired, it was perhaps a bit *too* niche for the majority of my peers. It's likely that they were more interested in watching puppets career about in crazy cars and crack scatological jokes than analyse the mechanics behind it all.

And whilst the backstage sections are unabashed fun, the general emphasis of the show is skewed too much towards an audience that probably wasn't watching. Buckley concedes that the show wasn't quite as well formed as he had hoped:

"I can't pretend the show was a massive hit with the viewers, who didn't quite know what it was. An exec at the BBC said to me afterwards "I wish we'd made it, we would have refined the idea and got you a second series". I think that's true, but with ITV being more ratings conscious (because of the advertising) it was a case of if it's not a clear hit, let's ditch it and try something else. I did think there was more of the world of puppets to show, but we had almost exhausted the inter-puppet chat show format with Billie I think."

Nonetheless, the very fact that you're reading this book is proof indeed that it's a show for you and Buckley sums up its charm thusly:

"What was most striking was the way that the crew fell in love with so many puppet characters, or appreciated the skill involved in making and performing puppets. It was, and remains, the ability of these funny little characters to make us believe they're alive – if only for a moment – that never ceases to make me smile."

TEDDY EDWARD

BBC1
1973

Technology may advance at a rapid pace and fads may come and go, but teddy bears remain a resolute pillar of childhood; their furry, almost stately charms are hard to deny, so it's understandable why so many children cling onto their beloved teddies in bed and well into adulthood.

And it's not only in reality that teddy bears are cherished, fiction is equally as obsessed with these woolly-haired and adjustable limbed caniforms. Children's fiction, in particular, takes great delight in transporting teddy bears into a narrative and children's television has followed suit accordingly.

One of the lesser spotted teddy bears stalking through the vast forests of British children's TV is Teddy Edward, a medal wearing and globetrotting teddy whose adventures are captured in *Teddy Edward*.

The Bear Necessities

Narrated by veteran newsreader Richard Baker, *Teddy Edward* concentrates on the activities of Teddy Edward and his animal pals Snowy Toes the panda, Bushy the bushbaby and Jasmine the rabbit. A number of Teddy Edward lookalike teddy bears also pop up, but remain nameless.

Together, these characters set off on their travels to explore various parts of the world and their accompanying landscapes and phenomena such as rain, snow, fishing, red Indians and mountains.

These affable narratives are told through a series of still photographs which are zoomed in and out of to show the characters in their surroundings. No movement is present and, apart from Richard Baker's narration, the rest of the soundtracks consists of ambient sound effects e.g. birdsong and running water.

I know that description doesn't really suggest much of a visual picture, so let's take a look at the 'Visit' episode to establish what a *Teddy Edward* episode consists of.

It starts with Snowy Toes sailing down from his home in the mountains to see Teddy Edward; before Snowy Toes knows it, Teddy Edward has dug his fishing rod out and they're fishing. It's a sedate, peaceful scene, but this calm is soon interrupted when Teddy Edward gets a bite on his line.

There's such a struggle to land the catch that it must *surely* be a whale. Teddy Edward and Snowy Toes use all their might to wrestle and thrash with the line, but additional help is required – cue the arrival of several Teddy Edward lookalikes.

Eventually, the catch is landed, but it's not a whale. Instead, the denouement of the episode is a world away from Moby Dick as Teddy Edward has actually caught a bell. However, far from leaving Teddy Edward with the bitter taste of failure in his mouth, he's very pleased as it's a very fine bell indeed.

A Bear's Tale

Teddy Edward started as a series of books written by Patrick Matthews in the early 1960s and were inspired by a teddy bear that Matthews' daughter Sarah owned. The idea to photograph this teddy, stemmed from a photo that Matthews had taken of Cecil Beaton's cat in a flower bed – yes, really. Matthews and his wife, Mollie, then wondered whether there was something in photographing their daughter's teddy bear and telling stories around it.

The resulting Teddy Edward books sold around 250,000 copies and led to the BBC considering a TV adaption in 1965, but the idea failed to gain momentum. Following Matthew's retirement from the world of publishing, he approached the BBC to discuss the possibility of adapting Teddy Edward's adventures for TV.

Perhaps regretting their decision in 1965, the BBC offered Matthews thirteen five-minute episodes in the *Watch with Mother* slot. The series was not an in-house production by the BBC and, instead, came from Q3 London who also produced *Fingerbobs, Crystal Tipps and Alistair* and *Joe*. Richard Baker was brought in following his previous children's TV voice work on *Mary, Mungo and Midge* in 1969.

Although operating on a fairly basic premise with no requirement for a film crew – Matthews took all the photos himself – *Teddy Edward* was certainly not made on a shoestring due to Teddy Edward's reputation as a "much travelled bear" with production trips to Spain, France and Greece.

Only one series of *Teddy Edward* was produced, but it was repeated up until 1978 and also aired in New Zealand and Norway. Following the end of the series, a number of books and records were produced to continue the adventures of Teddy Edward such as Teddy Edward Goes to Mount Everest.

And you may be wondering where Teddy Edward,

himself, is now located. Well, following Matthews' death in 1996, Teddy Edward was sold at auction to a Japanese collector of teddy bears, Yoshihiro Sekiguchi, for £34,500 and ensured that Teddy Edward embarked on at least one more grand journey.

Ready, Teddy, Go!

Despite not airing in over 35 years, *Teddy Edward* still holds a special place in the memories of many children. And, the fact that it was transmitted in amongst such classics as *Bagpuss* and *The Clangers,* inevitably means there must be something special tucked away in *Teddy Edward*.

Being born in the early 1980s, though, meant that I completely missed the *Teddy Edward* bus and, with available footage being limited to a few seconds at best, I was a little worried that it was a slice of children's TV which would remain out of my curious grasp.

Thankfully, the BFI Archive were able to rustle up two episodes – 'Visit' and 'The Farm' – of *Teddy Edward* for me to get a handle on the series and determine exactly why it's remembered so fondly by those who watched it in the 1970s.

First and foremost, the initial premise of *Teddy Edward* and its lack of movement may sound cheap and limited, but Patrick Matthews has managed to secure such an array of locations that the whole world appears to be Teddy Edward's oyster.

And these locations are so picturesque and pastoral that they're perfectly deployed to create peaceful, timeless environments which define the innocence of children's TV; it's an achievement which is further bolstered by Matthew's amazing photography.

Despite the opening theme being a jaunty, woodwind led affair, the actual soundtrack reflects the appealing photography by teasing out the gentle hum of nature. It's a collage of sounds so tranquil and relaxing that it clearly offers a less toxic alternative to drugs for treating insomnia.

In spite of this, it would be a foolish move to sleep through *Teddy Edward* as the gentle charms of the characters and stories tap into that irresistible British brand of delightfulness. And central to this is Teddy Edward himself.

Teddy Edward isn't a Holden Caulfield style character bursting with ticking idiosyncrasies and flaws; instead, he's the epitome of a warm, welcoming bear who exudes a simplistic allure at every turn, so it's no surprise that he surrounds himself with such equally agreeable friends as Snowy Toes.

And the plots these characters find themselves in are... well... they're not exactly overloaded with shape shifting narrative frameworks.

Teddy Edward hunting down an egg for his breakfast is far from eventful, but these are stories for pre-schoolers, viewers for whom damning indictments of religious faith – or concepts just as hideously grown up – can wait a few years.

Instead, the adventures of Teddy Edward are concise romps through an idyllic world which, regardless of being far removed from reality, are quintessentially British. They draw from that great tradition of children's stories which impart crucial life lessons through the exploits of the protagonists.

The icing on the cake is the charismatic voice of Richard Baker whose warming tones grant *Teddy Edward* a calming presence. It's a skill that Baker had honed in the newsroom and prevents any hint of panic ever setting in, so, in the end, you always know that Teddy Edward is going to be okay.

Grin and Bear It?

Teddy Edward absolutely deserves a larger mention in the history of British children's TV, but due to a relatively short run of repeats – compared to other shows – the series has never *quite* reached the upper echelons of its genre in terms of unadulterated fandom.

It's a real shame as here's a series which ticks all the boxes required to qualify as classic children's TV in such a unique manner. With its marvellous photography, charming characters and fantastic sense of Britishness, *Teddy Edward* has a lot to offer any newcomers to the party.

Teddy bears may, in conclusion, make unusual bedfellows – especially when their real life counterparts would rather savage us – but the eternal appeal of teddy bears means you'll never want to give up *Teddy Edward*.

MOP AND SMIFF

BBC1
1985

The human-animal bond is perhaps one of the most familiar, yet enigmatic social interactions we encounter on planet Earth. Humans develop emotional bonds with their pets which are akin to familial ties – we look after them, we play with them and we accuse them of hiding the remote.

Pets, though, are resolutely mute characters and they remain mysterious beasts at the best of times. As a result, we're keen to anthropomorphise them to understand their aloof ways and justify the huge level of moral care they receive.

It's a reductive process and one that, perhaps, we adopt in order to validate the effort we put into maintaining social connections with our pets. However, with the promise of a warm lap and a bowl of food never far away, pets are more than happy to be labelled as mini humans.

It's a win-win situation for both sides, so let's not get too cynical because it's a touching relationship. And, in *Mop and Smiff*, we see this age old friendship rightly celebrated.

Man and his Pets

Tucked away in the rolling Pennine moors is an idyllic village where the stresses of modern life feel a million miles away. Quintessentially British, it's a village where cheery window cleaners rub shoulders with farmers and gleeful children run amok as the seasons gradually shift through their respective gears.

And it's in this village that we find Mike (Mike Amatt) carving out an uncomplicated life against a rich tapestry of music and art with his shaggy Old English Sheepdog, Mop, and his purring tabby cat, Smiff.

The initial sections of *Mop and Smiff* feature Mike and Mop venturing out into the village to meet an array of characters at work (or play) in their respective trades such as guide dog trainers, farmers or even Mop's family.

Mike's friendly, inquisitive nature allows these lifestyles and characters to be gently probed as melodic songs unfold in the background to summarise these jaunts around the village. Smiff rarely features here, prone as cats are to their sense of independence and refusal to embrace the restrictions of a leash.

It's not until Mike and Mop return from their walk round the village that Smiff begins to get involved. Following a midmorning bowl of milk, it's time for Mop and Smiff to drift off into the land of nod, but this isn't the end of the story, merely the beginning of a new chapter.

This gentle slumber, you see, provides Mike the opportunity to paint the scenes of their dreams in an animated section where Mop (Timothy West) and Smiff (Prunella Scales) are granted the power of speech.

Sketching the Dream

Mop and Smiff was first broadcast in spring 1985 on BBC1 in the See-Saw slot as part of a 10 episode run, but three additional episodes aired in a repeat towards the end of the year.

Episodes, which aired in the lunchtime See-Saw slot, were 15 minutes long and produced by David Brown who was head of Children's Programmes at BBC Manchester. Brown was friendly with Sid Waddell – best known as "the voice of darts" on the BBC – and gave him the director's job. Amatt remembers the commissioning process as a fine experience:

"I married in 1975 and immediately after the honeymoon we bought Mop at a kennels in Lancashire, and the day after decided he needed a friend so we rescued Smiff from the cat shelter here in Bolton. Mop was so named because it is short and sweet and we knew he would grow into a shaggy mop coated adult.

Smiff was named after my friend's band who played at our wedding. For the next few years I continued to work as a cabaret act and on one of my trips to Lesotho Holiday Inn I became bored and homesick, so I wrote a story about Mop and Smiff.

When I had done that, I thought again that I should write songs about their antics. This was inspired by a cartoon that Harry Nillson wrote called "The Point". I sent a tape and some pictures off to a company in Walthamstow called "The Picsa Music Group".

They were making cassettes for small children. They liked my stuff so I went to them and we made four cassettes. This gave me a finished product that I later sent to the head of children's programmes at BBC Manchester, David Brown.

I was invited to the BBC to discuss things and I expected to be in for about 20 minutes. I left after about an hour and a half, walking on air. Another trip to Southern Africa, and I came back to a letter inviting me to a script conference.

Then things began to happen. When I realised we could have "names" doing the voices, I wanted Brian Glover to be Mop's voice and I wanted Polly James to be Smiff. David Brown met Timothy West and

Prunella Scales on a train to London and asked them if they would do the voices. They were wonderful in the studio and lovely people"

Mop, wasn't too concerned about the promise of a glittering TV career and decided that he would try and test the BBC's resolve as Amatt reveals:

"Some time before the transmission of the first episode, in April, I was invited to Television Centre to a press reception for all BBC kid's TV shows. Johnny Ball was there, I remember because we are both from Bolton. Anyway, sometime during that day, my wife and I, with Mop, were waiting on the 6th floor of the big round building.
We were outside a room which had "Director General" on the door. Immediately outside the DGs office, Mop decided to take a pee on some of the plants. There was no stopping him. Fortunately nothing went on the floor of the corridor. Nobody knew this happened"

Despite Mop's unpredictable bladder, *Mop and Smiff* went out as planned and there was even a spin-off series in the form of *Mike, Mop and the Moke;* this was a very different show which found Mike and Mop travelling round seaside towns and playing games with children. Notably different to *Mop and Smiff*, it featured neither Smiff nor any animation. Despite *Mop and Smiff* being repeated for several years there was never a re-commission as Amatt discusses:

"When the people at the top at the BBC move on… so do their underlings. Staying in favour at the Beeb was like climbing a greasy pole. Even before I had children of my own, I came to the conclusion that almost all kids shows are made by people with no children. It's still the same. I could create and present better formats etc. today but who wants *to know an old bloke? Telly is a fickle industry"*

Dream a Little Dream

With his engaging personality in full throttle, Mike Amatt is the epicentre from which all of *Mop and Smiff's* brilliance emanates. Mike's blessed with a gregarious nature and it feels like a symbolic link to his serene surroundings. Straight away, you find yourself relaxing as Mike bounds out his house with the ever loyal Mop at his side.

Accordingly, it would be foolish to complain that Mike's adventures around the village aren't packed full of exciting *Die Hard* style set pieces. Popping down the post office for chocolate drops isn't exactly Bruce Willis in a vest, but *Mop and Smiff* is aiming more for Mike Amatt in a bobble hat. Children find wonder in the most simplistic and everyday scenarios, so this approach pays dividends in *Mop and Smiff.*

This wondrous world is pushed into even more sublime territory with the cracking soundtrack Mike provides. Mike's musical background is firmly shored in the 1960s and 70s, so it's no surprise to find him crafting shimmering melodies that recall The Beatles and The Kinks at their reflective best. These songs drift gently across the moors infiltrating every crack of life that Mike explores and even seeping into the dreams of Mop and Smiff.

Mike, naturally, is not marketed as the star of *Mop and Smiff,* that's the job of Mop and Smiff, so how do they fare? Well, in their mute, live action form, they're always going to struggle to engage the viewers. Mop does his best to transcend this by displaying a sense of loyalty and an intense level of cuteness, best demonstrated in one scene where he leaps joyously through swathes of bracken in slow motion. Smiff makes little impression in these sections, limited as she is to a few brief scenes indoors and around the periphery of the house.

The animated sections of *Mop and Smiff* provide the chance to anthropomorphise the pair, so it's here that their characters start to flesh out a little more.

Not surprisingly, the furry duo feel like an extension of Mike's personality, shot through, as they are, with an intense loyalty and inquisitive innocence. Special mention must be bestowed upon Timothy West and Prunella Scales for helping to tease these traits out of Mop and Smiff with an ease that underlines their experience.

Built upon simple narrative foundations such as chasing butterflies, sledging on rolls of carpets and sniffing out a pie at the circus, the animated stories aren't exactly pushing the boundaries of storytelling. However, there are just enough knockabout japes and scrapes to secure the wayward attention of a child for five minutes. And whilst the animations aren't intricate pieces of art, they're big and bright which, again, tie in with the simplicity of the show.

Two of a Kind?

Although *Mop and Smiff* may not provide any startling sociological insights into the human-animal bond, it's a sweet reminder of the simple pleasures our pets can bring us. And the rustic charm of Mike, Mop and Smiff's relationship is framed by a gentle introduction to the society around us.

It would be easy to argue that the world presented by Mike Amatt is too pastoral and idealised, but it would also be highly cynical. Misery may seem to pervade society, but *Mop and Smiff* is an elegant reminder of how humanity is nothing without the simple pleasures of life as Amatt reflects:

"I loved both Mop and Smiff very much. They both lived to be 14. Mop had a massive stroke one night in March and I had to take him to the vet to be put to sleep. I'd always had an understanding with Mrs Radcliffe whose farm we filmed the kite sequence on, that Mop could be buried there, and he was.

I was digging his grave as the sleet was coming at me sideways and tears and snot were dripping down my face. Smiff had died of kidney failure a couple of weeks earlier. She was buried in the family garden. On March 24 my first son was born and we already had an 18 month old daughter... so as one door closes... another opens and life goes on"

RUNNING SCARED

BBC1
1986

I've only ever walked through the Woolwich foot tunnel once – about 25 years ago – but the haunting memories it evokes are still crystal clear in my mind's eye. The seemingly never ending length – tough work at 8 years old – was permeated by gloomy lighting and the rather disturbing knowledge that the murky River Thames was only a few feet above.

It had a nightmarish edge to it, the kind of place you'd expect to be chased by a serial killer. Whilst you had a broken leg. And the gates at the end were locked. By Satan himself.

By a stroke of luck, no harm came to me that day, although I did get a little out of breath. Despite this revelation, I was still rather relieved to make the return journey via the Woolwich Ferry.

Not everyone in the foot tunnel, though, emerges unscathed by its dramatic potential. And, just a few years earlier, a young girl had been subjected to a terrifying chase down the foot tunnel by an East End villain in *Running Scared*.

Trouble in East London

Life for a girl in mid 80s Britain is a tough old task. Not only is there the constant romantic anxiety about boys, but there's also the struggle to find space on bedroom walls for posters of Wham. Paula Prescott (Julia Millbank) has both these problems *and* a further complication in the form of respectable businessman cum East End villain Charlie Elkin

(Christopher Ellison).

Club owner Elkin is your stereotypical ne'er do well who, when not traipsing around the golf course, has plenty of dubious past times. This makes him of particular interest to D.I. McNeill (James Cosmo) who would be as pleased as punch to put Elkin behind bars. And it appears that Elkin may just have made a slip up of monumental proportions.

Following an armed robbery, Elkin and his heavies experience a bit of motor trouble, so are forced to hightail it from the scene in a taxi driven by Paula's granddad – Sam (Fred Bryant). In typical getaway fashion, the rules of the Highway Code aren't adhered to and a rough journey ensues. In the hullabaloo of an emergency stop, one half of Elkin's broken spectacles find their way under the taxi and into McNeill's evidence room. The other half remain in the taxi and are swiped by Sam.

After Paula is threatened by Elkin's moll, Leila (Hetty Baynes), Sam realises just how serious matters are. And, not wanting to be slung in Barking Creek himself, Sam has to concede that it's better to let sleeping dogs lie.

Following a sinister late night warning from Elkin, Sam changes his mind and decides to play his hand against Elkin. Knowing he has the upper hand with the glasses, Sam warns Elkin off his family, otherwise Sam's half of the glasses will end up in McNeill's hands.

Sam's time on Earth, however, is limited due to poor health and, just before he passes away, Sam advises Paula that his old musical box holds an important message. Elkin, meanwhile, has cottoned on that Sam must have left a message about the whereabouts of his glasses and is determined to find it.

Luckily, for Elkin, he has an inside track to Paula through her cousin Brian (Simon Adams) who just happens to be one of Elkin's goons. And Brian's shady activities aren't limited purely to family betrayal. He's also helping to terrorise Paula's Sikh friend, Narinder (Amarjit Dhillon) and her family over 'protection' payments for their printing shop.

Running up that Hill

Running Scared was a six part series which aired on BBC1 in early 1986 and was the final part of the Children's BBC schedule on Wednesdays. The show was the product of esteemed children's novelist, Bernard Ashley, who was, at the same time, also holding down the rather taxing task of being a head teacher.

Interestingly, *Running Scared* was not based on an original Bernard Ashley novel, but was especially written for TV. A tie in novelisation was released following the series' transmission.

The series scored a real coup when Marilyn Fox came on board as director; you only need to take a quick peek at the shows she directed (*Earthfasts, Five Children and It, Codename Icarus*) to understand the astounding talent she possessed for crafting very special TV. Keeping the majestic vein of experience flowing was executive producer Paul Stone whose career also took in *The Box of Delights, Moondial* and *Jossy's Giants*.

These two masters of production were tasked with bringing Ashley's vision to the screen, but what exactly was this vision? Well, the narrative itself was based on personal experience and set within a recognisable landscape to the author as he explains:

"When I was writing 'Running Scared' I was living, as I still do, in Charlton, a couple of streets away from where I was born in Woolwich. But the story's main influence was from my job between 1971 and 1977 as head of a large three-decker multi-racial school in Newham, There was a strong Sikh community in the area, and we had a Sikh member of staff Riat Singh who became a friend.

The 'inspiration' for the plot – if not for the themes in 'Running Scared' – was a musical box left to me by an aunt. As a writer of thrillers – which describes the genre of many children's books – I explored ways in which I could use that musical box as a plot pivot.

Newham is just across the free ferry from Woolwich. I've known the ferry since a child, and with the drama of its churning water behind the paddles and the foot tunnel deep underneath its route, I wanted to use them in the serial, both had dramatic possibilities. Apart from some shooting at the Thames Barrier on the south side of the Thames there were no other south London locations as far as I know"

Running Scared was also unique in that Marilyn Fox managed to secure the recently released Kate Bush single 'Running up that Hill' as the theme tune.

On the Run

Being only three years old when *Running Scared* first aired, I was a little too young to catch it and, accordingly, I'd never heard of the serial. Fortunately, I seem to have been blessed with an uncanny knack for discovering curios of British TV, so it was no surprise I would bump into *Running Scared* at some point.

And, sure enough, a chance search through YouTube brought me face to face with a children's show which featured Christopher Ellison; I was immediately sold.

What really endears *Running Scared* to me is the kaleidoscopic view of the grit and grim making up the underbelly of this East London narrative. It's a territory where physical violence tussles with organised crime and makes for some arresting viewing.

And whilst *Grange Hill* endeavoured to provide a similar dose of realism, it never felt this adult; especially when *Running Scared* serves up the sight of Hetty Baynes swanning around in a swimsuit. The content may feel near the knuckle for children's TV, but Ashley recalls no problems with the powers that be:

"I wasn't aware of any problem of getting 'Running Scared' on the screen. Under the overall management of Anna Home, head of BBC Children's Television, I worked with Head of Drama Paul Stone throughout. Every couple of weeks I drove to BBC Elstree Studios (parked in what was the Grange Hill 'playground') and we took the story on.

So far as I knew, at no point did anyone question what went on the screen. When Anna and Paul had commissioned me it was on the back of the sorts of books they knew I wrote. My only slight disappointment was when I wanted Charlie Elkin to pursue his gentrification by joining an Essex hunt, but being shown-up there by one of his 'heavies'. That would have been too expensive to film so he joined a golf club instead"

Running Scared certainly pulls no punches, but Bernard Ashley is still able to weave a story where its central themes are subtly integrated. The scripts manage to sow the seeds for a diverse range of lessons which are indispensable in the healthy upkeep of a child's moral rectitude as Ashley recalls:

"I didn't consciously set out to make young viewers aware of the serial's themes of friendship, family, honesty, anti-racism or hypocrisy. They're simply there in the story as part of the fabric. I was aware, though, that I wanted the wider viewing public to know more about the way of life of a minority element in British society, and to appreciate its values."

The blueprints for the show demonstrate the ambitious nature flowing through its veins, but once the actors step in front of the camera *Running Scared* really comes to life.

Julia Millbank and Brian Butler both provide lively and mature performances, so it's a shame their acting career never flourished as they seem dead certs for *The Bill* or *EastEnders* on this showing.

Christopher Ellison was born to convey all the seductively dicey traits of society and he's on terrific form, although, at the initial read-through, he suggested Bernard Ashley should be playing Elkin! Hetty Baynes also delivers a tremendous performance by injecting a sinister dose of psychopathy into Leila which threatens to surpass even Elkin's ruthlessness.

And, as the serial comes to a close, James Cosmo – who's impressive as ever, but sadly underused here – sums up this superb upgrade of children's TV with the final line of "That'll do nicely",

Scared No Longer

Running Scared rightly refuses to sanitise its tale of urban crime for children's TV; this creates a thrill for the young viewer as they're treated to the exciting opportunities of adult TV in their own backyard.

It's an important position for the show to take as it taps into the audience's transition into adulthood. A noteworthy addition to the canon of amazing yet unheralded children's TV, *Running Scared* makes me want to head straight for Woolwich and take on the foot tunnel once more.

LET'S PRETEND

ITV
1982 - 89

Adults need all manner of material distractions to briefly escape from reality, but young children don't have access to credit cards and, as a result, have to find joy in other places. Thankfully, children are blessed with the most wondrous creativity. And it doesn't cost a penny.

With a fertile imagination at their disposal, children can begin to explore the world around them all from the comfort of their bedroom. And with a few household props they can create practically any environment they like; if they've got a dressing up box and like to sing then it's even better!

Now, someone once said that "Talent borrows. Genius steals", so it's reasonable that children – little geniuses that they are – need a little bit of inspiration to cultivate their imaginative endeavours and, acting as the perfect creative springboard, they can find this in *Let's Pretend*.

Using the Imagination

Let's Pretend starts in a playroom, a wonderful playroom full of toys and instruments. And housed within this bastion of childhood delights are three 'pretenders' sat at a table. Talk soon turns to an object such as bubble mixture or a tablecloth and helps to kick-start the episode's theme.

After a bit of creative re-imagining of these objects – e.g. using a broom as a crutch – the pretenders decide that they're going to put on a play, but first they gather round a piano and bash out a song to really cement the episode's theme.

Two of the pretenders then take a short stroll across the playroom – the 'musician' pretender remains at the piano – and into the performance space, a sparse area populated only by soft, colourful lighting and a few props, but don't worry as a bewitching tale is on its way.

The plays take on plots which look at thirsty magicians conjuring up giant bubbles to secure some orange juice, doctors encountering incredibly accident prone patients and we're even treated to two posh twits stranded on a desert island in need of a paddle.

And, with the exception of the few props on offer, these plays rely on the pretenders' ability to pretend and improvise with each other and their surroundings. The plays are completed by revisiting the original song from the playroom and brief highlights from the play for the viewers to focus on.

Behind the Pretence

Let's Pretend was part of the lunchtime schedule on ITV between 1982 – 89 with 207 episodes being produced by Central Television over an eight series run. Unfortunately, the entire first series is officially missing, but at least one episode – 'The Garden Bench' – is believed to be held in an arts archive.

Legendary children's show *Pipkins* had previously occupied the *Let's Pretend* slot, but due to a change in ITV's landscape, something new was required as writer Gail Renard recalls:

"Sadly Pipkins ended when ATV lost its franchise – which we

never thought for a moment would happen. Central TV was the new ITV franchise holder and wanted to own its own pre-school series and start afresh. Pipkins' producer, Michael Jeans, asked Pipkins' writers Susan Pleat, Denis Bond and me to write the new series, Let's Pretend"

The team's aim was for *Let's Pretend* to stimulate the fertile imagination of the young, lunchtime audience as Renard explains:

"*Children love pretending and it's important that they're encouraged to use their imaginations. They can find fun and fantasy in everyday objects they see around them. A canister Hoover with a long hose can look like an elephant if you stick ears on it. Kids also love stories and music so we wove them all into Let's Pretend. There were also educational elements too*"

The initial concept of *Let's Pretend* may have originated in amongst the neurons and synapses of Michael Jeans' mind, but Renard remembers the entire creative team getting involved with the development of the show:

"*Michael Jeans created the main format but Susan, Denis and I were always very involved with the production. We'd have storylining days together when we'd put together all of our ideas, develop them and see which ones we wanted to turn into episodes. It was fun and there were no egos. We were always generous with each other. If someone really wanted to do a particular storyline, we were happy to say it's yours.*

We also attended the studio recordings. Writers really need to, especially on a long running series. You need to see the actors' strengths so that you can play to them in future, as well as what might not be working so well. You also suddenly get new ideas when immersed in it all"

One notable element of *Let's Pretend* was that – despite some regular pretenders such as John Telfer, Kerry Shale and Martin Smith – there was no definitive lineup in place as Michael Jeans was reticent to rely on any one performer. As a result, dozens of actors passed through the doors of *Let's Pretend* and Philip Bird, who appeared in several episodes, remembers his time on the show fondly:

"I had presented some episodes of Merry-go-Round, a BBC programme for children, and had worked for ATV (which became Central) on Sapphire & Steel and the final Callan. Maybe one of those helped get me seen. Derek Barnes was the casting director on Let's Pretend. I guess he called my agent and invited me to meet Michael Jeans. I was asked to write a song and come in and play it on the piano. The brief for the song may well have been for it to be about an elephant who can or can't dance.

Anyway, I brought a pair of wellington boots and played the song on the piano, with occasional clumpy pirouettes in the gaps in the music. I don't remember any song of mine being rejected by him, and the rest of the cast were always encouraging and supportive. We worked as a team, throwing in ideas whenever they occurred to us. Time was fairly tight so the work was concentrated. John Telfer is a great, talented man. Andrea Gibb is now also a writer. Hardly surprising, given her inventiveness"

Sarah Lermit – who appeared in two episodes following her graduation from drama school – also remembers her involvement with *Let's Pretend* as being a creative and challenging experience:

"The initial brief required me to be able to sing and dance and play various parts within the episode; I had to come up with some creative ideas with the other actor and the musician and improvise so that we could then establish a story and firm up a script. As I said, it was a creative process, so there was a lot of work and pressure in the rehearsal studios to come up with a good story and to tell it in an amusing and entertaining way.

On set, when filming, you ran from beginning to end with no cuts if I remember right and it was quite complicated to do. All the costume changes for the different characters you were playing – and getting the props in the right place at the right time – were all done in real time, so it was pretty full on and nerve wracking for a novice actor!"

John Telfer, one of the longest serving pretenders, recalls an equally enjoyable introduction to the series:

"I was in very first series and I was sent up by my agent for this television interview with Michael Jeans – a lovely man, completely off the wall, like a bumbling professor – and Chris Hazell the musical director who occasionally appeared as the musical presenter.

And it was a really nice interview, I remember that Michael said "Draw me a silly pink elephant" so I did a quick scribble. The next day, though, I had a think about it and decided I could draw a better picture, so I sketched a dancing elephant and sent it to Michael. And I got the job"

The actors involved in the series were also given the opportunity to help shape the stories into their finished form as Telfer explains:

"Michael set a very open process of rehearsals. Some of the scripts were very tight, but some were of variable quality, so we'd throw them around a bit more to get the best out of them. We had three lots of rehearsals (in Camden) before recording at the end of the week (originally at Elstree and later Birmingham). You had to decide on the characters very quickly and this wasn't always easy as, for example, one episode I was playing a fried egg and a boiled egg – Bobby the Boiled Egg and Frankie the Fried Egg. Frankie turned out to be a real slippery, sexy character!"

Despite the show's long lifespan, the format changed very little with only the opening credits changing. Originally, a conveyor belt would transport the episode's props (a la *The Generation Game*) towards the crunching jaws of a shark-like creature. After the first series, Michael Jeans decided this was a bit too ferocious for pre-schoolers, so the *Let's Pretend* caterpillar was introduced. Early series had this puppet caterpillar dancing across the screen before being revealed to be operated by one of the pretenders. Later series would have a more generic opening where the caterpillar, in a succession of costumes, would wriggle around an illustration of the *Let's Pretend* house

Relying on Creativity

Ah, *Let's Pretend*! Now there's a children's TV show which had a significant impact on my way of viewing the world when I was knee high to a grasshopper, well, I was probably just under one metre, but let's not get too pedantic, okay?

Yes, so, *Let's Pretend*, what was its effect upon my tiny brain? Well, inspired by the antics of the pretenders, I decided, one afternoon, to play *Let's Pretend*. And, strapping on my older brother's rucksack, I pretended the stairs in my hallway were a mountain and set about scaling them.

There's no way I would have even contemplated such an exploration of my imagination without *Let's Pretend*. With its influence ingrained upon my temporal lobe, it's no surprise that this vivid memory of the show has refused to vacate the older recesses of my memory.

My initial introduction to *Let's Pretend* was 30 years ago and due to a lack of repeats I hadn't seen the show for nearly as long. Could *Let's Pretend* still pack a punch and inspire my sense of wonder all these years on?

Despite the long lifespan of *Let's Pretend* – and falling comfortably within the era of home recordings – very little footage is freely available, so all I could find were a few clips which failed to tell me the whole story. Eventually, I managed to secure a private viewing from a kind friend and I then found that the BFI held two episodes, so I set off to digest the lot.

And, as those gentle, dreamy piano tones kicked in, I was transported on a crescendo of melody back to an era where all I had to worry about was where I would set up my base camp on the stairs. Matters had got off to a good start, but what would lie within *Let's Pretend?*

Now, the first thing to address is the *Let's Pretend* caterpillar puppet that appears in the opening titles as it's one of the strongest memories for many viewers. And, it's fair to say, their memories of this little red and yellow larva are enshrined in nightmare inducing territory.

However, I'm not entirely sure why as he comes across as a curious and playful fellow who's keen to embrace the pretending ethos of the show by dressing up. Okay, I guess the strange, synth based noises he makes are a little disturbing, but it's nothing to hide behind the sofa about.

With this 'horror' quashed, it's time to move onto the core concept of *Let's Pretend*. And, like all the very best children's TV, it's a concept which grasps simplicity close to its heart. There's no need to complicate matters with various frills and distractions, instead, the power of creativity is entwined into the show's heartbeat.

What's clever – and most important for *Let's Pretend* – is the show's ability to show young viewers that you don't need elaborate sets and props to perform and tell stories. Sure, it would be lovely to provide every child with a huge wardrobe and an on hand set designer, but that's not feasible.

Dispensing with the need for a budget, when the pretenders transform the blank canvas of their performance space into any location that their play demands, it demonstrates to the young viewers the huge potential of their imagination and what it can achieve.

The plays themselves have plenty to impart to the young viewers and consist of life lessons, humour, singing and silliness, so it's the perfect formula for engaging children. It never falls into the trap of coming across too overbearing and the plays are all helped, of course, by the fantastic pretenders.

The enthusiasm with which the pretenders perform is matched only by their acting talents, so this helps bring the plays to life and gives them an exuberant feel. There's a fabulous section in a series two episode where John Telfer, Steven Mann and Martin Smith all sing 'Row, Row, Row Your Boat' in a round style and it's so infused with actorial charm it's difficult not to admire their brio.

And it's no surprise to hear that Telfer has nothing but

fond memories about the recording of the series:

"We all loved Michael, he had a wonderful grandfatherly presence and was endlessly good humoured which made for a wonderful working atmosphere. You had your favourite people you worked with, I had lovely Tessa Hatts and Aidan Hamilton. In fact there was one clip of myself and Tessa playing an octopus, Tessa sang testicles instead of tentacles and we fell about in hysterics. It ended up on one of those TV Blunders shows, it's been shown three times, so we've been paid for it three more times!"

The final aspect of *Let's Pretend* which makes it a special show is the huge number of pretenders involved in the series. By constantly serving up so many new faces, *Let's Pretend* is able to remain fresh and not rely on any one performer being the life-force of the series. It's a move which affords *Let's Pretend* yet more originality and when you consider the quality surrounding it, you'd be hard pressed to find any reason to begrudge the show its eight series span.

Pretender to the Throne?

Let's Pretend is a marvellous dose of lunchtime children's TV which manages to cram a level of quality into the production which appears to defy the laws of physics. This is no surprise as the whole point of your creativity is that it can stick two fingers up to the petty restrictions of physics.

Imagination is crucial to *Let's Pretend's* success as it provides a firm footing for the young viewers to get involved. It's delivered with an admirable ease, has a marvellous set of performers and a highly experienced creative team to thank for achieving this.

And whilst my 'mountain climbing' experience didn't lead to me becoming an actor (or a mountain climber), it was one of the many influences which showed me how something could be created from nothing, hence this book. It's an amazing feat to transcend the TV schedules and become inspirational, but one that ensures *Let's Pretend* will never be forgotten.

ALFONSO BONZO

BBC1
1990

When you're a kid, mastering the art of swapping is essential when it comes to achieving your materialistic dreams. After all, there's always something your mate's got that you want and vice versa. Cold hard cash is a scarce asset for kids, so the long, arduous process of saving those pennies and pounds means swapping is the most immediate and straightforward option to hand.

Nonetheless, swapping isn't as simple as it sounds. Even the most talented swappers can come to discover that it's a dangerous path to traverse. In fact, in *Alfonso Bonzo* we're privy to a cautionary tale which demonstrates just how far reaching the ramifications of a simple swap can be.

Swap Shop

Billy Webb (Scott Riley), now there's a veteran and somewhat master of the old swap scene. With a magisterial touch, young Billy is able to negotiate amazing swaps on all types of crazy items with the residents of Splott Street and his mucky fingered school mates at Splott Junior and Infant School.

Billy's swaps make him popular with his peers, but his propensity for swapping anything drives his Mum (Susan Porrett) and Dad (Brian Hall) nuts. Nonetheless, although they may be irritated by Billy swapping his jumper for some old Elvis LPs, nothing's going to prepare them for Alfonso Bonzo.

Alfonso Bonzo (Alex Jennings) dresses with a continental flamboyance and his arrival is always heralded by a jaunty whistling, but who is he? Well, he's an Italian exchange student, but he's not coming over here to learn about our culture and nick your dad's cigarettes. No, he's come to perform outlandish and otherworldly swaps with Billy Webb.

Now, Billy may be the best swapper in the Splott district, but Alfonso comes ready packaged as the market leader of swapping. And each swap he offers to Billy promotes a fevered reaction to its potential. Want a magical bag? Alfonso's got one! Want a talking dog? Alfonso's got one! Want to traverse the dimensions of space and step directly into your TV? That's right, see Alfonso!

Naturally, Billy can't resist these swaps, but maybe he'd be better off with the mediocrity of swapping football stickers; this is because the greatness that Alfonso's swaps promise is counterbalanced by their wildly unpredictable nature. Billy, therefore, begins to uncover a hidden subtext that the grass isn't always greener on the other side.

The whole story is told in flashback by Billy who is now holed up in hospital with a broken leg. He's laid up next to journalist Trevor Trotman (Mike Walling), who also has a broken leg and is enthusiastically convinced that Alfonso Bonzo is proof of extra-terrestrial life.

Behind the Swaps

Back in those halcyon days of 1986 not only did we have the release of The Queen is Dead and the sublime genius of Maradona at the Mexico World Cup, but we also saw the release of the children's book Alfonso Bonzo by Andrew

Davies.

Davies is best known for his TV adaptations of *Pride and Prejudice* and *Vanity Fair*, but he was also the master behind one of the most underrated sitcoms ever, *Game On*. Anyway, Davies realised that he had created a story which was just perfect for the small screen, so he set about adapting it for TV.

Alfonso Bonzo first aired in January 1990 on BBC1 in the 4.30pm slot in the Children's BBC schedule and ran for 6 episodes. The series received just one repeat, about 18 months later on BBC1 again. Billy Webb, meanwhile, went on to have further adventures in *Billy Webb's Amazing Stories*, but this was sans Alfonso.

Life Swap

Alfonso Bonzo passed me by at the time, but as luck would have it, one of my mates was a keen fan of the show. They implored us to delve into the show and give it the once over, so I duly started some groundwork on it.

On discovering that *Alfonso Bonzo* was one of Andrew Davies' babies, I was absolutely sold and powerless to resist investigating it. To make matters easier, the whole series was on YouTube, so I eagerly hit the play button.

The first aspect I need to address is Billy Webb's constant reference to Alfonso as a "mad Italian hippy". This is incredibly harsh as Alfonso is far too dapper to be reduced to a mere Mediterranean counterculturist. In fact, if you can imagine a late 1980s Italian take on Doctor Who then that's *exactly* what Alfonso is. And whilst there's a whiff of the Milanese catwalks about Alfonso's attire, Alex Jennings manages to dress the character with even more layers of class.

Alex Jennings has won three Olivier Awards and, based purely on his *Alfonso Bonzo* showing, it's impossible to question these decisions. He's astounding in the role of Alfonso and he lights up the screen with his unstoppable charisma every time he saunters into view. No wonder Billy's Mum and sister go all giddy over him.

Talking of Billy Webb, I can't overlook Simon Riley's performance as the lovable little oik. Blessed with a seemingly never ending palette of incredulous expressions, Riley provides a fine performance opposite Alfonso's brilliance. His range is impressive for a young actor and he can ably turn on a sixpence from humour to cynicism to intense frustration. Sadly, it appears that Riley didn't fancy the career of an actor as his acting CV is far too short.

The main narrative thrust of *Alfonzo Bonzo* centres on Billy and Alfonso's complex relationship, so the rest of the characters are very much bit players. However, this doesn't mean their acting should go unheralded. Sadly taken from us far too young, Brian Hall brings his infectiously likable Cockney air and comic timing to Billy's Dad. And Bryan Pringle, as headmaster Mr Hardwood, conjures up his trademark stern, authoritative persona, but one whose icy heart is quickly thawed by an Italian greyhound.

With all this high praise lavished on the performances, the story's going to have a tough task to match them. Now, I can think of children's TV shows with more clever and ingenious plots, but *Alfonso Bonzo* is one for whom the cerebral willingly steps aside for madcap fun.

It's laced with the unabashed excitement which is quintessential of mid-afternoon children's shows, but the tone gradually evolves as the story unfolds. The narrative begins with a chirpy if uneventful energy, but this is merely the calm before the storm; Alfonso's entrance leads to a crushing crescendo of chaos as his swaps are let off the leash.

Alfonso Bonzo is cleverly incisive at getting to the core of some important themes for its viewers. Children tend to overlook the virtue of contentment as the world is a relatively new environment for them. And, much like a moth drawn to a flame, they can't help but reach out to the danger on offer despite the risk of getting singed. Circumstances prove, for young Billy, that being mindful of shiny objects dangled tantalisingly close is an important lesson to learn.

The one minor quibble I have with the show is the flashback structure employed to play out the story with hindsight. Don't get me wrong, Mike Walling is a fantastic comedy actor and he's bubbling away with a comedic vim and vigour, but the main narrative is strong enough to dispense with any clumsily tacked on exposition.

Fair Swap?

Ultimately, *Alfonso Bonzo* is a show which takes an eccentric look at why children should put some time aside to ground themselves in reality. Children, though, have notoriously short attention spans, so managing to keep them sedentary long enough to absorb these lessons is a tough task.

Nonetheless, Andrew Davies seems to manage it with ease with a script and performers that I wouldn't swap for the world.

BRIC-A-BRAC

BBC1
1980, 1982

Bric-a-brac shops always held a certain allure for me as a child. First off, there was the alliteration of the name which rather tickled my prospering aural receptors. Secondly, there was the strange clutter to sort through whilst I rummaged for Dr Who Target novelisations. Finally, there was also a small chance that I might bump into Brian Cant, the Don of children's television and, in particular, *Bric-a-Brac*.

Open for Business

Housed within the dusty depths of a bric-a-brac shop, in amongst a plethora of even dustier curios, lives the elderly, nameless and slightly dusty shopkeeper (Brian Cant). Possibly stripped of his sanity by being enslaved to a shop which experiences no passing trade, the shopkeeper has developed a passion for phonetics.

Each episode of *Bric-a-Brac* finds the shopkeeper becoming fixated on a particular letter of the alphabet and its pronunciation. This phonetical infatuation inspires the shopkeeper to comb the shop in search of items which will authenticate the existence of these phonemes e.g. the B (buh) episode finds the shopkeeper piling up the following bizarre combination: a bear with bananas in its mouth as a bucket stands by with a brolly in it.

Stocktaking

13 episodes of linguistic intrigue were produced by the BBC over the course of two language obsessed series in the early 1980s. Michael Cole – a man blessed with an almost supernatural talent for developing timeless TV – helped to create *Bric-a-Brac* with one of the great children's TV producers, Nick Wilson. The magnificent roll call of talent continued with the appointment of Cynthia Felgate (*Play School, Play Away* and *Willo the Wisp*) as executive producer.

Bric-a-Brac – not to be confused with the similarly titled BBC1 1970 antiques TV quiz show – aired as part of the glorious See-Saw lunchtime roster and episodes lasted roughly 10 minutes. Each series was repeated multiple times through the 1980s with the final repeat being broadcast in September 1989.

No commercial releases followed and only a couple of episodes have emerged onto YouTube over the years, but I was able to catch up on a few more episodes at the BFI Archive.

Alliterative Magic

Bric-a-Brac was one of those shows that my memory refused to erase all traces of. My recollections of the series still felt fully formed and these were no doubt borne from the warm, nostalgic memories of curling up into the crook of my Mum's arm as we watched Brian Cant potter about.

Now, unless you're the chairman of the clueless goon society, you should be well aware that Brian Cant is one of the godfathers of British children's TV. I'm not saying that he's prone to cutting off horses' heads and sneaking them into Cosmo and Dibbs' bed, but more that he appeared in a wide range of pioneering and influential shows such as *Play School, Play Away* and the *Trumptonshire* trilogy.

And *Bric-a-Brac* finds Brian Cant on sparkling form. His avuncular nature is so perfectly formed and suited to *Bric-a-Brac* that I wouldn't be surprised to discover that he had been created in a test tube by a perfection seeking BBC executive.

Yes, his talent is that outstanding and it's reflected in the manner he disregards the limitations of being a solitary performer in *Bric-a-Brac*. Cant manages to bounce off the viewers, the objects in the shop and even his own absentmindedness to build an energising rapport which has a vice like grip that clamps its teeth firmly around your temples.

And the alliteration that Cant gets to twist his tongue round is monumental. The 'R' episode finds him coming back from rambling with the Red Rovers Rambling Society and, of course, he has Rick Robinson's rucksack as Rick refused to go rambling because of the rheumatism in his right leg. Taking this linguistic exercise even further, the rucksack contains a raincoat, a roadmap, a roast beef roll with relish and radish, some Roman relics and a collection of rocks (a round rock, a reddish rock and a rough rock).

The letter P meanwhile sees Cant looking after Pretty Polly the parrot for his friend Peter who owns a petshop and has gone to Porto, a particularly pretty place in Portugal. And the parrot seed for Polly goes behind the parrot perch on the piano with the peanuts. I could probably run through these all day as they're so much fun, but I'll stop here, although, as a final treat, I'll inform you that G sees Cant with a gate he's got off his friend Gus from Grantham that he's planning to clean all the grime off with some gubbins.

The scope of the phonetics theme is fairly simple, so avoids falling into the trap of dispensing a gruelling dose of education. Thankfully, due to the myriad of peculiar objects creating a sense of intrigue and wonder, the audience is blissfully tricked into learning about the words gurgling out of their mouths.

And the final touch of brilliance comes when the episodes quite literally wind down; the shopkeeper digs out an ancient clockwork toy which he leaves running over the credits. These toys – donated by the Worthing Museum – include a rascal rapping a rat, a person on a pig which spins round and a leaping tiger named Genghis Khan. And the manner in which these toys gradually wind down is an astute allegory on not just the transient nature of the shop's contents, but life itself.

Worth a Rummage?

Despite a premise which I have to admit looks ridiculously limited on paper, *Bric-a-Brac* is another example of Michael Cole's talent for summoning up brilliant TV from a shoestring budget.

Aided and abetted by the magnetism of Brian Cant, it soon becomes clear that, in practice, *Bric-a-Brac* is an engrossing watch. It may not be scintillating, it may not cover the entire alphabet, but it's a gentle reminder that, with a warm heart at its centre, a TV show can cut through the decades to retain a timeless charm.

ROUND THE BEND

ITV
1989 - 91

Being a child provides you with the wonderful opportunity to be as juvenile as you please; it's a privileged position and one that you lose as you get older. When you're nine years old, no one bats an eyelid if you run round the playground screaming about bums, but you try that in your early 30s and people get frightfully judgemental.

Whilst this behaviour is frowned upon in adults, children are allowed to get away with it as it's considered "just a phase". However, not only can this "phase" last a lifetime and provide a blueprint for comedy, but, it also acts as a useful testing ground for how society tackles taboos.

And, sometimes, the best way we can tackle taboos is by embracing them and removing the fear factor which labels them as something we couldn't possibly discuss. Children, of course, aren't too bothered about the mechanics behind this, they just want to drive you *Round the Bend*.

Sewerage Silliness

Deep down in the twisting, cavernous tunnels of the sewer system, there lies a dank, dark epicentre to all that is silly. And the man, or should I say aquatic reptile, in charge is Doc Croc, a shirt and tie wearing crocodile who acts as "The fun loving, friendly editor of Round the Bend, the world's first electronic video comic".

Joining Doc Croc, and helping to produce Round the

Bend, are three rats whose treatment at the vicious, lashing tail of Doc Croc severely stretches his definition of "fun loving" and "friendly". Nonetheless, when you discover how frustrating and inept these rats are, you begin to empathise with Doc Croc and find new respect for his lashing tail.

Middle class rodent reporter Jemimah Wellington-Green is eternally failing in her quest to secure a celebrity exclusive, whilst the terminally cheerful 'comedian' Vaudeville Vince Vermin has more cringeworthy jokes than you can shake a stick at and, finally, in Luchetti Bruchetti, we have an Italian artist and the preferred whipping boy of Doc Croc.

Together, this disparate bunch of characters encounter all sorts of chaos and hijinks down in the sewer; Doc Croc runs for Parliament on behalf of The Greedy Party, Vince's tiresome penpal Eric Postlethwaite pays a visit, the rats form mega-band The Rattles and there's a time for a killer teddy to run amok (twice).

The first series also sees Jemima attempting to conduct interviews with celebrities such as Tony Robinson and Aswad. Making her way through the sewers, Jemima emerges headfirst from these celebrities' toilet bowls, but rather than welcome her with open arms, they flush her away in disgust.

Equally disgusting are the pop stars who visit each week to perform their greatest hits, but look a little closer and you'll realise they're not quite what they seem; pile of snot Sneezy Wonder sings 'I Just Called to Say You're Mucus' and actual toilet Elton John belts out 'I'm Still Smelly'.

And, being an electronic video comic, there are, of course, animations. Lots and LOTS of animations.

Keen on parodies, *Round the Bend* takes great delight in skewering childhood favourites such as *He-Man* (Wee-Man and the Masters of the Looniverse), *Thundercats* (Thunderpants) and *Transformers* (Transformaloids – Totally Useless Objects in Disguise). Children's TV in general is also parodied in the form of original animations including the peculiar bodied 'OddBods', insane hypnotist/magician 'Pzycho the Magnificent' who's constantly being arrested and 'Kenny McTickle and His Magic Kilt' which is more than capable of conjuring up Jason Donovan.

There's also time films to be ruthlessly ribbed and torn apart before being reconstructed with a healthy dash of silliness, so this is why we're treated to Ricky VIII (*Rocky*), Arizona Jones and the Scroll of Destiny (*Indiana Jones*) and James Bomb – Licenced to Hurt (*James Bond*). The world of claymation is also embraced to bring weekly serials to *Round the Bend* which heavily ape 50s B-movies in the form of 'False Teeth from Beyond The Stars', 'Attack of the Atomic Banana' (filmed in Bananarama) and, finally, 'False Teeth from Beyond The Stars meet Atombanana'

Creating the Bend

Three series of *Round the Bend* aired on ITV between 1989 – 1991 with each series consisting of six 20 minute episodes. The first two series went out on Friday afternoons, but the third series found itself sitting in the Monday schedules. A few years later, the series was repeated on Channel 4 and The Children's Channel.

The seeds of *Round the Bend* were sown in mid 80s anarchic kids comic Oink! which included the characters Tom Thug and Horace 'Ugly Face' Watkins. Created by Tony Husband, Patrick Gallagher and Mark Rodgers, Oink! ran for 68 controversial issues before declining sales brought it to an end.

Despite the controversy, Oink! was highly popular with its readers and hadn't gone unnoticed by the world of television. Yorkshire Television were keen on adapting Oink! for the small screen and, as Tony Husband explains, the end result was *Round the Bend:*

"We knew that Oink! was fading and was going to be pulled and, all of a sudden, this guy from Yorkshire Television came to us and said they wanted to do a TV version of Oink! They said 'We want a version of Oink! with animation, a TV version and we'll make you an offer you can't refuse'.

And this offer was absolutely abysmal and we rejected it straightaway, so they made us another offer which was equally abysmal and we didn't know what to do. We didn't want to sell it cheap and we didn't own the copyright, IPC did and they had ties to Robert Maxwell.

By chance, we had a meeting with Denise O'Donoghue who had just started Hat Trick Productions and was interested in new ideas. We went down to see Denise, Rory McGrath and Geoffrey Perkins who said to forget Oink! as Maxwell would bleed us dry, so we went away and came up with Round the Bend.

At the time, Hat Trick were on the upsurge, so we got Spitting Image involved, John Henderson the director who knew everyone and Catalyst Pictures who were based just down the road from me in Ashton (which was convenient) and we just started writing.

The Hat Trick guys wrote with us to start with – Jimmy Mulville, Rory and Geoffrey – and guided us on how to write for television. We had so many ideas that they just left us to it eventually – for every show we had about 10 minutes extra material as we were so prolific.

And we were lucky that Hat Trick managed to broker a deal with

Yorkshire Television which gave us a budget of around £500,000 per series"

The writing process behind *Round the Bend* had been honed on Oink! so Husband, Gallagher and Rodgers were all aware of each other's strengths and Husband remembers this being key to the series' success:

"*We all wrote individually and then had meetings to put it all together. Patrick worked in London – he was more of a set designer and worked on all the cutouts – so I remember me and Mark doing a lot of the writing, but sometimes we got behind.*

I remember writing a whole program – one about elections – on my own whilst the others were catching up and filling in on the ones we were behind on. So it was a very democratic co-operative group of us. And, just like Oink! we were a fabulous team who all knew our parts.

Bob Painter at IPC once said to me "What I love about you three is that there's no ego between you". If we came up with an idea we loved, but the other two didn't, we wouldn't sulk as it was a democratic thing and we trusted each other. We all had our own way of thinking, a bit like Monty Python I suppose"

Round the Bend was also blessed with a supporting crew of some repute. Many of the puppeteers had recently worked on David Bowie classic *Labyrinth* and Nigel Plaskitt – stalwart of quality children's TV – also contributed his puppetry magic. The puppets, themselves, came courtesy of the Spitting image crew.

For Patrick Gallagher, working with the Spitting Image team was very exciting, but *Round the Bend* also represented a chance for Gallagher to succeed in a manner he had long dismissed as possible as he recalls:

"It was an incredibly exciting time for me. I'd always wanted to work in TV but having left school at 16 with only two O levels, plus a kick up the arse off the headmaster, and subsequently having not been through college or university, I never thought a career in TV would ever happen. Also, I was a big fan of Spitting Image, so it was a dream come true when they were commissioned to make Doc Croc and the live action puppets to my designs.

I was allowed great creative control right from the start, since the character and set designs I'd developed for the pitch document were instrumental in the commissioning of the series.

However, at the time I put the document together, I always thought that if the show was commissioned and went into production, a more experienced TV designer, such as Tony Hart from Vision On, would be appointed to develop the characters, but fortunately that never happened.

Consequently, and further down the line, I overlooked the 2D animation in Manchester at Catalyst Pictures, whilst producer and director John Henderson - fresh from directing Spitting Image - took charge of the 3D animation in Bristol, which was produced there by Aardman Animation's Dave Alex Riddett, of Shaun the Sheep and Wallace and Gromit fame"

Going Round the Bend

An incredibly silly child – I once spent an entire year's worth of school lunchtimes pretending to be Sherlock Holmes working on a case against the nefarious 'mice women' – *Round the Bend* seemed custom made to burrow deep down into my psyche and celebrate its passion for the ridiculous.

Now, aged eight years old, I struggled to even spell

parody, let alone comprehend the mechanics behind a swift lampooning. Be that as it may, there was something exciting about *Round the Bend's* subversive approach to children's TV and popular culture which introduced me to a new strand of comedy.

And it made such an impact on me – almost certainly influencing my dalliances with the world of Sherlock Holmes – that my memories of the show remained fond and vivid. Nonetheless, whilst the mere idea of Thunderpants still tickled me, it was time to reappraise *Round the Bend*.

On the surface, *Round the Bend* appears to follow a fairly generic framework applied to numerous Saturday morning children's magazine shows; this is a shrewd move by the creators as it not only provides a familiar format, but also allows for a variety of sections to be parodied.

It's a parody which is heavily backed by an incredible sense of humour and one that resolutely fails to stray into the ordinary. For example, even though a cartoon entitled Weeman and the Masters of the Looniverse should, on its own, be funny enough, the writers push it to even more ridiculous extremes by featuring characters such as Rock Bottom – literally a bottom made of rock.

And even the more dramatic features in *Round the Bend* still refuse to be compromised by any sense of maturity. False Teeth from Beyond the Stars, for example, appears to be a gripping B-movie, but still finds time for the false teeth to pause their megalomaniac schemes in order to watch *Neighbours*. And then complain when it's postponed due to the cricket.

The comedy, as I'm sure you've guessed, is thick and fast, so, although the series apes the structure of a Saturday morning children's show, it's much closer in spirit to a sketch show. As with all sketch shows, not everything succeeds, but *Round the Bend* has a hit rate which puts most adult shows to shame.

Backing up this high level of quality, the running times for each segment are pleasingly concise, with very little (the serials aside) running for more than 90 seconds. Therefore, if you're not being entertained by the Oddbods, then Thunderpants will have you rolling on the floor before you know it.

This variety in content is also matched by a wide range of illustrative styles which prevent the different segments all merging into a monotonous stream. Due to the different styles of the creators, these styles can verge from loose, cartoony aesthetics through to highly stylised drawings. The final designs were overseen and created by Gallagher as he explains:

"I was responsible for every design and style element of the show, including the Round the Bend logo, the puppets, the animation characters, the main sewer set, the end credits (which I hand drew personally) and all the graphic props used on set during filming.

The only elements of the show that I didn't design were False Teeth from Beyond the Stars and Attack of the Atomic Banana, the 3D animations which Dave Alex Riddett at Ardmann Animation produced. Though in the proposal document, I did include a design of mine for the demonic false teeth"

Steeped in juvenile humour, *Round the Bend* is pleasingly crude what with its emphasis on bottoms and bodily functions, so it's refreshing to actually revel in this without any recriminations of taste. And, I was surprised to discover from Husband that they received no complaints:

"No, no complaints whatsoever. None that I heard of anyway, unless Yorkshire Television dealt with them. And Hat Trick were always very good at dealing with that sort of thing. It was just slapstick and silly, mad but fun. Oink! had loads of complaints and upset a lot of people, but Round the Bend didn't"

There were certainly no complaints forthcoming from the studio floor as Gallagher remembers:

"It was electric! I was really flattered to hear that the puppeteers, who'd all been involved on The Muppets and Spitting Image, thought Round the Bend was something really special. They all loved the characters they operated and worked incredibly hard to bring them to life, adding their own little quirks and idiosyncrasies along the way.

In between takes, Anthony Asbury, a formidable Texan who operated Doc Croc (and also Spitting Image's Maggie Thatcher), kept up the pretence and stayed in character mode with Doc, even though the cameras weren't rolling. Doc would hurl abuse at director John Henderson and anyone else that caught his cantankerous crocodilian glance as we prepared to go for another take.

It was incredibly rewarding to work in an atmosphere of such camaraderie and fun with a team you had the utmost respect for. I would have actually paid to have been there (which Doc actually suggested at one point)"

After three series, Round the Bend sadly came to an end and I always remember being disappointed that I wasn't going to get my fix of Doc Croc et al. Husband remembers being ready for furthering the adventures:

"There was some sort of contract between Yorkshire Television and Hat Trick, but the fourth series never arrived even though we were ready to go; it was a big hit at the time, it was a very expensive series to make, so this may have contributed".

Gallagher, meanwhile, is convinced that *Round the Bend* could still work in this modern, more sanitised era of television:

"I think Round the Bend could still work on TV today with its deliberate subversive and anarchic attitude, obviously with more contemporary references. Thinking about it, we might come under attack from the PC brigade, particularly if we still referred to the audience as 'Benders'.

In a way, Round the Bend was ahead of its time on many levels. It was billed as 'The world's first electronic video comic', decades before the advent of multimedia digital publishing"

One to Flush?

A unique presence in children's TV, *Round the Bend* is an amazing production which stops at nothing in order to elicit those huge belly laughs. Oh, sure, it's puerile and it's a perfect example of why many parents wouldn't let their children watch ITV (yes, this actually happened), but the way in which it careers headfirst through any boundaries of taste is quite thrilling.

The sheer weight of anarchy and subversion at the heart of *Round the Bend* could easily feel overwhelming, but instead it produces a rush of excitement that gets the blood pumping and sends colour to even the most pale and wan cheeks. There's a non-negotiable pursuit of the viewers' attention and, at the end of it, *Round the Bend* has well and truly won.

ORM AND CHEEP

ITV
1984, 1987

The animal kingdom struggles to live in perfect harmony. Cats hate dogs, birds can't help but gobble up worms and wasps have a zest for hating everyone. Despite this innate hatred, there's proof that certain groups of animal can put their differences aside in the quest for a more fruitful connection as seen in *Orm and Cheep*.

When Animals Live Together

Cheep is a fluffy little bird who, after falling from his nest as a baby, fails to learn the basics of being a bird - namely being able to fly. It's a potentially tragic introduction to life, but wriggling about on the edges of this narrative is the friendly worm, Orm. Rescuing Cheep from the unforgiving digestion processes of the food chain, Orm takes Cheep back to his subterranean home at the base of a tree.

Together with their friends Snail, Mole and Mouse they deal with such testing situations as cleaning the house, coping with floods and allowing Cheep the freedom to express his artistic talent. To add an extra dimension of urgency to these plots are their enemies Crow, Cat and Rat who are keen to establish the predator - prey relationship that Orm and Cheep have rejected.

Behind the Puppets

Orm and Cheep started to come to life when writer Guy Hallifax was introduced to designer Tony Martin. An idea for a children's TV show had been burrowing away in Tony Martin's mind for some time, but scripts were needed. With Guy Hallifax on board the scripts soon became a reality and, before the pair knew it, they had a commission from ITV. 26 episodes of *Orm and Cheep* followed over the course of two series between 1983 and 1985.

The puppets populating *Orm and Cheap* were created by The Puppet Company and their world was a mixture of backdrops created by Tony Martin and bluescreen magic engineered by Derek Oliver. Bringing an established, calming presence to the proceedings was Richard Briers with his cheery tones which provided the whole gamut of voices and narration for the series.

The fractious tensions of a marriage in breakdown between Jan and Tony Martin could have left the production swinging a noose up to the rafters, but the pair's ability to limit conflict prevented it from dominating the production.

By the time of the second series, Jan Martin had checked out of the production team. Any thoughts of a deep seated spousal feud are firmly undermined by Jan Martin's positive comments about her ex-husband's work on the series.

Orm and Cheep was highly successful at the time and managed to make a real connection with its viewers; it's no surprise that a wealth of merchandise followed. Six tie-in books were released along with an *Orm and Cheep* annual whilst The Video Collection released a VHS featuring 5 episodes of *Orm and Cheep*.

Turn the Cutesy up to 11

There's a special place in the landscape of children's TV for puppet shows. Endearing characters are brought to life with furry limbs against a canvas of relatable themes for children. As a child, I was smitten with TV puppets and it felt as if marvellous creation after marvellous creation was raining down heavily from the TV heavens.

I never caught Orm and Cheep, so it was ripe for an investigation. A rip of the VHS release has found its way online, so I loaded it up and prepared myself for the unknown.

As the cutesy, saccharine theme tune began to emanate from my laptop speakers I was struck by an intense wave of nausea. I found myself aggressively questioning just who could conceive such sickly pretensions. Imagine a nightmarish world where Keith Harris had turned to Orville and suggested that they wring a little more soppiness out of 'I Wish I Could Fly'. Be under no illusions, this chilling vision is made real by the *Orm and Cheep* theme tune.

Once the muscle contractions of my gastric system had rescinded, I pushed onwards with my exploration of the show.

First things first, Richard Briers was a national treasure thanks to a cheery disposition which he distilled into an art. By some feat of Darwinian evolution he also arrived with inexplicably perfect oral rhythms.

And in *Orm and Cheap* he uses these to provide a warming articulation to his narration. Combined with the soothing background music provided by Dave Greenslade, it makes for an unmatched smorgasbord of aural delights.

With the perfect soundscape in place *Orm and Cheep* has a solid bedrock, but would the puppets match this quality?

Sadly, they're a frustrating element of the show. Orm and Snail keep the cutesy factor of the protagonists on track with their slick design, but Cheep lets the side down by appearing to be a rushed ball of glue and feathers. Meanwhile, the sinister intentions of Cat and Rat fail to manifest themselves in their design, so it's a struggle to differentiate between the two groups.

A mixed bag of puppets can easily be swept aside by wonderfully vibrant plots populated with outstanding characters. Unfortunately, this isn't the case in *Orm and Cheep*. My main gripe with the good guys is that they emerge as overglazed, hollow characters who are sickeningly polite. Such insipid characters put a real strain on the already paper thin plots, so I found my enthusiasm for them rapidly draining away.

And, as the credits rolled, I felt cheated that Orm and Cheep's idiocy and doe eyed naivety hadn't resulted in them being gobbled up.

Is it Over Yet?

Beamed through the innocent retinas of a toddler, *Orm and Cheep* does actually contain some pearls of wisdom. The fundamental basics of society are clearly laid out and teach crucial lessons on friendship and the triumph of good over evil.

However, to my weary, thirty-something eyes, the lurid, schmaltzy world of *Orm and Cheep* is far too sanitised and the whole thing feels like a missed opportunity.

CODENAME ICARUS

BBC1
1981

Science is a magnificent enterprise which has helped us develop new technologies, make exhilarating postulations about the universe and even clear up athlete's foot. And we're all exposed to it at school for several long years – science that is, not athlete's foot – so we're more than capable of holding a little scientific wizardry in our brains, even if it only amounts to working a bunsen burner.

However, some of us – not me obviously – are right science whizz kids and can answer fiendishly complicated scientific riddles to help advance mankind. Are these advances always put to good use though? It's a complex question and certainly not one that can be answered in a book examining the stranger corners of retro TV, but we can take a look at a TV program which questions this in *Codename Icarus*.

A Hidden Genius

Thanks to his nonchalant approach to studying, Martin Smith (Barry Angel) isn't exactly in the running to be crowned 'student of the year'. Bubbling away beneath this exterior of dismal grades, however, is an exciting streak of genius.

And this high intellect reveals itself when Martin solves a perplexing equation with complete ease. Rather perversely, the school believe it's far too outlandish an achievement for the doltish Martin, so, at first, he's branded him a cheat.

When Martin's not rolling his eyes at his academic tutors

for their inability to handle him, he spends his free time hunched over a school computer solving difficult equations posed by an enigmatic question master. This veil of secrecy soon drops to reveal that John Doll (Philip Locke) has been setting these equations to verify Martin's genius.

Doll is part of the Icarus Foundations which runs Falconleigh School and specialises in nurturing child prodigies. With the approval of his family, Martin is soon channelling his brilliance at Falconleigh.

There's something dark and strange going on behind the scenes at Falcolnleigh, though, and Martin's natural curiousity refuses to let this lie. As he begins to uncover a systematic campaign of abuse against his peers, Martin soon finds himself being hypnotised, drugged and put through the psychological wringer.

It all seems to be in order to isolate Martin from reality and twist his genius to Doll's own nefarious needs, but can Martin get to the bottom of these schemes before it's too late? And just who is the mysterious Edward Froelich (John Malcolm) who's lurking behind the scenes at Falconleigh despite being presumed dead since World War 2?

Meanwhile, Britain's defence systems find themselves in a precarious position as an unknown assailant is ruthlessly sabotaging them. Watching through closed fingers, Andy Rutherford (Jack Galloway) has to witness test missile after test missile being blown out of the sky with childlike ease.

Unable to pinpoint the source of this aggression and, therefore, preserve the sanctity of Britain's defences, Rutherford finds himself suspended by his boss, Sir Hugh Francis (Peter Cellier).

Espionage, as we're well aware, is Rutherford's raison

d'etre, so he embarks on a freelance mission to uncover the truth behind these attacks. Luckily, for Rutherford, he just happens to be pals with ex-Falconleigh pupil, Frank Broadhurst (Gorden Kaye), who certainly knows his onions when it comes to the type of advanced laser techniques required to bring down a missile.

And is it just possible that the answer to Rutherford's quest could lie within Martin's struggle with the powers that be at Falconleigh?

The Inner Workings of Icarus

Fresh from penning ITV children's show, *Quest of Eagles,* Richard Cooper set about fashioning *Codename Icarus* in 1981 with the prodigiously talented Marilyn Fox (*Running Scared, Seaview, Jackanory*) directing the series with her fastidious skill. Curiously, *Codename Icarus* is one of those rare children's shows to feature a scientific advisor in the credits, Professor John Taylor, who I suspect had a brain the size of Saturn.

Barry Angel, who had previously appeared in *Agony* and *The Professionals,* remembers the filming process and team fondly:

"I was doing quite nicely as a young actor and got an audition for this role at the BBC. It was a great role for me at the time being the lead in a 'serious' children's series. Most of the filming was done on location around Andover in Hampshire and at Dunsford Airfield near Cambridge.

This was a great adventure for me; at 19 you're pretty fearless and I remember enjoying it immensely. It was a little strange filming things out of sequence but again, no fear! I was looked after really well by the

producer Marilyn Fox. The actors, too, were really good to me, particularly Jack Galloway and Gorden Kaye.
I learned a lot about how TV worked. It was interesting to learn how to film out of sequence and that taught me something about concentrating on where you 'were' each day. It built my confidence as the reviews, as I remember them, were pretty good. I think it was something a little unusual for children's TV at that time"

Codename Icarus first aired over a two week period in December 1981 with episodes airing on a Tuesday and Wednesday evening at 5.10pm on BBC1. A repeat airing – and the only ever repeat – came in spring 1984. A VHS compilation of the series was released by the BBC in 1985 and a region 1 DVD release eventually followed in 2006, but, as of writing, a region 2 DVD release is yet to surface.

Flying High with Icarus

I was happily whiling the hours away by brushing up on the life and times of Gorden Kaye when I stumbled upon one of his earliest roles. Entitled *Codename Icarus* it immediately conjured up visions of Gorden Kaye heroically sticking his boot into the Hun on D-Day – a somewhat proto *Allo, Allo* if you will.

After reading a little further I realised there would be no Fallen Madonna with the Big Boobies in *Codename Icarus*. Instead, it sounded like an epic vision which threatened to puncture the sky with its grandeur. And, as luck would have it, the whole series was up on YouTube.

If there's one thing that puts me off a retro children's TV show then it's a cavalcade of wooden performances. And it's not just child actors who contribute to this, even adults can phone in stiff, lifeless portrayals (see *Doctor Who* in the 1980s). *Codename Icarus* rebels against this limpness and generally manages to deliver a level of performance which elevates it above its peers.

Sure, Martin looks like a forgotten Britpop frontman, but he's brimming with depth and Barry Angel displays this precocious integrity with ease. It could be argued that, at times, Martin's a grouchy, misanthropic type, but what teenager isn't? And it's even easier to argue that Angel should have had a longer acting career ahead of him, but his life took a different path as he explains:

"I did one or two decent things but looking back I didn't have the drive needed to succeed and I just got fed up in my mid-twenties being either on the dole or working at low paid jobs to pay the rent and bills. I was a good cook and I took myself to college to study to be a chef, which became one of my many careers till now. I have no regrets – all a great adventure starting from the age of 16 as a Manchester school boy"

Meanwhile, Jack Galloway keeps the protagonists high calibre of performance flowing and his handsome looks imbue Andy Rutherford with a rugged charm and steely determination – the very blueprint of heroic espionage.

On the other side of the fence, of course, we have those moral miscreants, the villains. John Doll is sinisterly calm and Phillip Locke captures his psychopathic predilections through a mixture of chilling smiles and dismissive eyebrows.

John Malcolm, as Edward Froelich, also brings a bewitching performance to *Codename Icarus* and depicts his character's flawed logic with incredible authenticity. Gorden

Kaye is the weak link in the antagonists' chain, but this is due to his character, Frank Broadhurst, not being given much to do apart from sport a cardigan and clasp cups of tea.

It's when actors are handed an excellent script that they really start to shine. And *Codename Icarus* finds itself founded upon an amazing script by Richard Cooper. It's an intelligent script, *really* intelligent, and Cooper's love of narrative clout produces a children's show which is complex yet accessible.

Other thrillers from this era, which target an adult demographic, fall, all too often, into a series of mind-numbingly cerebral political discourses. *Codename Icarus*, though, manages to pull off that rare feat of keeping brains and action on an equal footing.

Concepts such as free will, child abuse and cold war paranoia are explored over the course of the script, so it demonstrates Richard Cooper's (and the BBC's) fantastic trust that a young audience could process such harrowing topics.

The main question that the show asks is whether the gift of genius should be forcibly manipulated or frittered away in blissful ignorance. Through science, man has the ability to right many wrongs in the world, but this can be at the expense of true freedom. It's a complex paradox and one that I suspect many children would have struggled to identify.

What's also strange for a children's TV show is the heavy presence of adults throughout the serial. Rutherford's plot strand is almost exclusively the preserve of adults, but rather than alienating the young audience, his espionage antics provide an exciting dose of danger and action.

It's also vital to keep *Codename Icarus* grounded in reality and not traverse the stereotypical path of the kids saving the day. Martin's genius is all well and good, but in reality, one child can't defeat wicked adult guile on their own. And that's why Rutherford's experience is essential in thwarting Falconleigh.

Nonetheless, Martin plays a key role in the series' denouement as he goes head to head with Froelich in a tour de force debate on the ethics of science. Froelich's attempts to justify his ambitions by revealing he sabotaged his genius to prevent the Nazis developing nuclear weapons, but by now he's babbling.

With an incredible level of irony, Froelich now believes he has his own final solution. Martin passionately denounces Froelich's twisted vision of a 'free' society and leaves Froelich crestfallen as he realises his grand scheme is over. It's one of the most important and powerful scenes I've ever seen in children's TV and makes for a fitting conclusion.

Higher than the Sun?

Codename Icarus left me speechless in terms of its sophistication and scope; it's difficult to comprehend all of these wonders without viewing the series, prone as we are to expecting unflinching simplicity from children's TV. And by broaching such intellectual themes and radical angles for such a young audience, *Codename Icarus* deserves to be held up as a landmark piece of British children's TV.

HEGGERTY HAGGERTY

**ITV
1983 - 84**

Magic is an art which challenges the boundaries of reality and confounds any expectations that our general understanding of the world can provide. It promises so much and appears to offer a more exciting way of life, so why isn't it more prevalent in our everyday lives?

As I'm sure you know, magic is just like a salesman's patter – all an illusion. Still, it's nice to dream and if there's one place you can dream and get away with it then it's within the confines of fiction. Hence, the plethora of stories going back thousands of years which embrace magic at their core.

And for children – who, on the whole, still haven't got to grips with dynamics and relativity – magic remains particularly attractive as there's little to prove otherwise to their immature, yet wonderfully innocent logic e.g. if a caterpillar can turn into a butterfly, why can't a witch turn a man into a frog?

Despite many witches in children's literature being seen as figures of wickedness and evil, some are more than friendly. And a fantastic example of being far too busy dealing with mischievous broomsticks to build gingerbread houses and roast children in the oven is *Heggerty Haggerty*.

Brewing up a Spell

Heggerty Haggerty is a kindly witch who does her best to live a peaceful, gentle life in her idyllic cottage with Black Cat and

Broomstick. Maintaining this bucolic living is severely tested by the impish antics of Broomstick who throws caution to the wind when it comes to magic.

And if Broomstick would only consider the ramifications of meddling with magic, perhaps Heggerty Haggerty wouldn't find herself confronted with whirlwinds, giant (and tiny) geese and running shoes with a mind of their own.

As well as calling upon her mastery of magic, Heggerty Haggerty is also helped by Farmer Giles and Constable Short to restore a healthy balance of normality. Black Cat, meanwhile, is keen to observe and voice his anxieties about the chaos beginning to unfold.

The show is presented and narrated by George Cole who appears in front of illustrations of Heggerty Haggerty's cottage alongside a few props such as a rustic country wall, a washing line full of pyjamas and even a single feather. Cole regales viewers with these tales of magic over a series of illustrations depicting the action.

Stoking the Cauldron

Produced by Yorkshire Television, *Heggerty Haggerty* was a lunchtime ITV show broadcast between 1983 – 84 with 26 episodes airing over two series. During the initial run, a 4pm repeat followed the lunchtime edition; a number of episodes were later repeated towards the end of 1985.

The show was produced by the multi-talented actor, puppeteer and producer Nigel Plaskitt whilst Alister Hallum directed. The beginnings of the show came from a simple dose of inspiration and some good old fashioned luck as Elizabeth Lindsay recalls:

"Like many good ideas, Heggerty Haggerty popped into my head when I was walking in the New Forest. Luckily, Yorkshire Television were looking to fill a slot where a programme had fallen through and Joy Whitby, the producer, loved the idea. Encouraged by Nigel Plaskitt, I got to work writing the stories and, together, we submitted them to the high-ups at Yorkshire Television. Getting the series commissioned was, for me, pain free as, in those days, once you had the support of an executive producer they glided you through the process!"

Joy Whitby was also key in two of the most crucial aspects of *Heggerty Haggerty's* production as Lindsay recounts:

"Getting George Cole involved was a real coup for the series. Joy Whitby was able to book him when he had a few days to spare – very lucky! Peter Rush provided all the illustrations and had previously worked with Joy Whitby. Peter was the perfect illustrator and worked fast"

Following the end of series two, there were no further episodes and Elizabeth Lindsay can't remember any discussions regarding a third series. A VHS release of 5 episodes followed in 1986, but the biggest impact that *Heggerty Haggerty* had was upon the career of Lindsay:

"Up until the point that I wrote the Heggerty Haggerty stories, I had only ever worn a scriptwriter's hat, but that soon changed; Scholastic Children's Books published several Heggerty Haggerty stories as picture books and I was then commissioned to write other stories for them with new characters.

Heggerty Haggerty began my prose writing career and I went on to write The Midnight Dancer, Magic Pony the Nellie and the Dragon series for Scholastic and The Silverlake Fairy Stories for Usborne Children's Books"

Riding the Broomstick

Keen to explore any avenue of British television featuring George Cole, I didn't need much convincing that *Heggerty Haggerty* was worth investing some time in. And when I discovered that it was a lunchtime children's TV show there was no going back. Luckily, I was able to track down a copy of the VHS release, so soon had five episodes to work my way through and see whether *Heggerty Haggerty* would leave me spellbound by its brilliance or mocking its magic thrills as nothing more than a cheap illusion.

George Cole had a fantastic voice which combined well-spoken thespian smarts with the engaging barrow boy charm that his cockney roots gave him. It makes for a charming and avuncular accent which is just perfect for narration.

And, of course, the action switches between the illustrations and the narration, so we get to see the great man in action. It's amazing that, by night, Cole was playing Arfur Daley, grumbling about 'er indoors and getting poor Terry into all sorts of bother, but, by day, it's a very different Cole.

Heggerty Haggerty is certainly no *St Trinians* or *Minder* masterclass in acting, just George Cole in a grandfatherly cardigan (he also slips into a tracksuit for one episode) talking to the viewer in a calming manner.

And this gear change in performance highlights Cole's versatility and his understanding of the series. It's more interested in focusing on the art of storytelling, so the show's energies centre on this rather than relying on Cole's natural charisma to drive the stories along.

Taking the mischievous Broomstick as a catalyst to conjure up tales of chaos and runaway magic, Elizabeth Lindsay immediately has the viewers on her side by providing a naughty little bugger for them to identify with. And what child doesn't delight in unhinged anarchy?

Nevertheless, the stories are keen to impress the idea that tampering with the unknown (on any level and in any setting) can have wide reaching effects. And that's why Heggerty Haggerty – with her adult control of all things magic – has to frequently come to the rescue with a quick spell.

Equally magic are the beautiful illustrations provided by Peter Rush. With simple outlines complemented by flourishes of detail, Rush lends the series his idiosyncratic style and breathes a further dimension of charm into the tales.

Spellbound?

Just perfect for the preschool crowd, *Heggerty Haggerty* contains everything that's required to make a sterling children's TV show. The importance of decision making and maturity with power is filtered through a funnel of surreal japes to keep the viewers entertained and leave them a little wiser.

It may be a relatively obscure gem of British children's TV, but thanks to the huge legacy left behind by George Cole and the appealing charm of its stories and illustrations, *Heggerty Haggerty* will continue to be remembered with great affection.

BEHIND THE BIKE SHEDS

ITV
1983, 1985

School days, are they really the best days of our lives? All I seem to recall is endless mornings and afternoons spent staring out the window of either freezing cold or swelteringly hot portacabins at nothing in particular.

Okay, I could have paid a bit more attention and actually done some of that there learning, but education can be such a frightful affair at the best of times, particularly when it's being enforced by a man for whom body odour and dental hygiene are foreign concepts.

However, it would probably have taken more than a swift shower and glug of mouthwash to liven things up and get me fully on board. What I wanted was a little bit more entertainment and, if I had known at the time, it could probably have been found *Behind the Bike Sheds*.

Please note that I'm not suggesting I could have found any French mischief behind the bike sheds. And certainly not with Mr B.O. Halitosis. It was just a little play on a schoolboy smut, anyway, back to *Behind the Bike Sheds*.

For Whom the School Bell Tolls

Series one of *Behind the Bike Sheds* finds the pupils of Fulley Comprehensive under the rule of headteacher Mr Braithwaite (Cal McCrystal) who bends his cane and swishes his black gown with all the dictatorial menace of Adolf Hitler – also the inspiration for Braithwaite's toothpaste moustache.

Perhaps the closest thing that Braithwaite has to an ally – and only because he's an adult – is Poskitt, the school caretaker. Poskitt may be a man of sartorial inelegance and lacking in IQ, but he's a friendly chap and rather nifty when it comes to tinkling the ivories and breaking into song.

Against this backdrop of adults, of course, there are the pupils in their delightfully pink uniforms, so let's take a look at them.

Adam (Adam Sunderland) is a plucky, fresh faced youngster whose main role is to open each episode with a narration on the current events at Fulley Comprehensive; he also acts as a springboard for updating and driving the plot throughout the episodes.

Joining Adam is his headphone wearing friend Paul (Paul Charles), a talented individual who can shift his feet like a young Michael Jackson, but also has aspirations of becoming a broadcast journalist as evidenced by his 'Jim Raving's Newsround' sections in series two.

Jenny (Jenny Jay), meanwhile, is a fifth-former blessed with a precocious savvy and a determination to highlight her singing skills which is matched only by her swooning passion for boys, particularly older ones.

Completing the pupils (well, as you'll discover in the following paragraphs, kind of) is Marion (Marion Conroy), a young punk bristling with attitude and a mocking wit which is curiously juxtaposed by her beautiful singing voice and twisting dance moves.

Whilst these pupils and adults all dwell above ground, there's one pupil (well, a puppet) who lurks eccentrically in the school boiler room and deserves a paragraph all of his own.

Injured and scarred by a radioactive school dinner in the Great School Canteen Disaster some years earlier, Fanshawe is a Phantom of the Opera type character who has failed to age since being struck by the offending school dinner. As a result, he keeps the Sacred School Dinner on the wall and worships it.

Going back above ground, the pupils of Fulley Comprehensive find themselves careering through songs and sketches on sucking up to parents and the horror of school uniforms. There's also time to squeeze in interviews with pop stars such as David Grant, Clare Grogan and The Thompson Twins.

Series 2 – with its change in writers – saw a change not only in cast, but also format. The pink uniforms were replaced by plainer uniforms, the pop star interviews shelved and the series became more of a musical sitcom with Braithwaite, Poskitt, Fanshawe and Marion all departing.

Replacing Braithwaite as headmaster is Miss Megan Bigge (Val McClane) aka Mega Pig, a clear parody of Margaret Thatcher and just as dominating. Despite claiming that she's a reasonable, loveable person who likes sweet children, she's actually a cruel, overbearing monster.

Keen to draw a line under Braithwaite's reign, Mega Pig claims to have the heads of Braithwaite, Poskitt, Fanshawe and the school cat Bonzo mounted on her office wall. The pupils are horrified by this disturbing sight, but Mega Pig discloses that they're just papier-mache heads.

Mega Pig needs someone to help hammer home her brand of sadistic authority and she hopes that the new deputy head Whistle Willie Jones (Ken Jones) is just the psychopath. Sadly, for Mega Pig, Whistle Willie is a wet blanket and is soon sacked, but he remains determined to prove himself.

More confident is Joe Winter (Tony Slattery) who arrives on a tidal wave of charisma, impressing staff and pupils. What Joe hasn't prepared himself for, though, is the level of anarchy awaiting him at Fulley Comprehensive which will force him through several personality changes.

And with the new gaggle of pupils joining Adam, Paul and Jenny, it's no surprise that Joe's mental resilience is on the ropes as he develops into a child hating maniac with fascist overtones (well, a Hitler moustache).

GBH (Linus Staples) is a thuggish, Mohican sporting punk with a penchant for cockney rhyming slang, and munching on PA systems. At the opposite end of the spectrum is Gertrude (Martha Parsey), a neatly dressed, polite goody two shoes. And, yep, you guessed it, GBH and Gertrude soon fall in love.

Chas (Lee Sparke) and AWOL (Andrew Jones) are a couple of likely lads who run many a dodgy scam and racket from the school boiler room. Chas is your typical cockney wide boy, all slick and confident whilst AWOL is a scruffy, slightly dirty lad from Yorkshire with a penchant for groan inducing gags.

With Marion gone, Jenny needs a new associate and in Skids (Julie MacCauley) she's got a new bestie. Skids has a natural talent when it comes to the old song and dance routines, but she's also a real sweetheart and even has a baseball cap with a toucan attached to it.

Skirting around the fringes of the schoolyard, the final character is Trolley Molly (Sara Mair-Thomas), a dinnerlady who carts her culinary wares around in a trolley. Although she has the look of a new romantic, her romantic visions are clearly aimed at Joe Winter, even selling 'jonuts' in his honour.

Preparing the Curriculum

17 episodes of *Behind the Bike Sheds* were produced by Yorkshire TV over two series between 1983 – 85 for ITV. The first series was written by Rick Vanes and John Yeoman, but the second series was written by Jan Needle with additional material from a young Tony Slattery.

A number of pupils featured in the series were restricted mainly to dancing (notwithstanding that some do get the occasional line) and these cast members grooved their way onto the set courtesy of The Harehills Dance Group.

Episodes aired during the 4.20pm slot with the first series airing on Wednesdays and the second series going out on Tuesdays. The series, as a whole, was never repeated, but the start of 1986 saw the transmission of five episodes entitled *The Best of Behind the Bike Sheds*.

Going back to the start of the series, Rick Vanes recalls that the original idea for *Behind the Bike Sheds* was inspired by his work on two previous shows:

"It evolved out of Ad-Lib and Sunny Side Up, on which I was script associate/writer. Both programmes featured groups of talented young people presenting items and performing sketches, and there was to have been a third series of Sunny Side Up.

Tragically, the director - David St David Smith - was killed in a helicopter crash while filming for a different programme, so Alister Hallum was brought in as producer/director.

He wanted to take the programme in a different direction, which I totally agreed with, and so we jointly devised the format that became Behind the Bike Sheds*"*

Due to the varied format of the series, writing Behind the Bike Sheds was not as straightforward as a standard narrative, but, as he explains, Vanes was lucky to be paired with an exciting writer overflowing with enthusiasm:

"John Yeoman was a talented writer who was relatively new to television, and the exec producer Joy Whitby wanted him to contribute to the series. He was London-based and I was in Leeds, so the process worked like this: Alister and I (plus Joy Whitby) decided on a theme for each episode - Parents, Fashion, Sport - and John and I, working separately, set about writing sketches and song lyrics based on the themes. I then stitched these together with linking sketches to create a vague flow to each episode. Although the lyric writing was shared, John wrote the majority of them. They were then set to music by Richie Close"

Vanes and Yeoman were also fortunate to be blessed with an excellent set of young performers to bring the scripts to life, something that Vanes was able to see up close:

"I was in the studio control room throughout the recordings in Leeds, in case last-minute tweaks were needed, but much more important was my attendance at the rehearsals in London. At the rehearsals I was able to pick up on some of the things that the cast were doing, and tweak, expand and cut things as the rehearsals progressed. The atmosphere was wonderful - probably the best I have experienced in any series. The cast and crew were like one big enthusiastic family, and everybody seemed to be having a ball"

Vanes and Yeoman's initial concept for *Behind the Bike Sheds* was markedly different come the time of the second series, but, as Vanes reveals, this is not a surprise due to the change in personnel involved:

"Joy Whitby, Head of Children's Programmes at YTV, and therefore exec producer on Bike Sheds, was hugely talented. But one skill she didn't have was the ability to trust in the ability of her producers and directors and leave them to get on with what they were good at.

She would constantly interfere and over-rule (sometimes with good suggestions, but sometimes not), and this led to a lot of friction between her and Alister Hallum - and when series two was being planned, she fired him from the show. I had huge sympathy for Alister and declined to work on series two because I felt he had been shabbily treated"

Back to School

Despite the boredom of school, it's a period of life which is so stuffed with formative moments that, even as we get older, ensures it remains a fascinating setting for a TV show. And, when I first heard of *Behind the Bike Sheds,* it was clear that here was a show for me to investigate.

However, after reading a little further, I was horrified to discover that it had strong musical elements. Immediately, I was confronted by troubling visions of dazzling smiles, tap dancing feet and all the other horrors associated with stage school pupils just itching to belt out Gee Officer Krupke!

Thankfully, the performers have the necessary skills to sidestep the pitfalls of stage school clichés and, instead, produce performances packed with youthful exuberance; it's a vibrancy which encapsulates that wisecracking, rough and tumble persona of British schoolchildren.

The pupils themselves are neatly divided into two subsections to help engage the viewers on different levels. Adam, Jenny and Paul provide a dose of child on the street reality to help narrate proceedings, whereas the comic flourishes of GBH, Chas and AWOL provide the schoolyard action.

Moving up the age groups, the adults attempting to instil calm and order at Fulley Comprehensive are equally as polished and well formed.

Braithwaite could easily fail as a caricature of disciplinarians, but little touches such as his meddling mother bringing him into school ensure he's fully three dimensional. Poskitt, too, transcends his berkish foundation thanks to his pride, misplaced confidence and ability to hold a tune.

Mega Pig receives the baton of crushing discipline from Braithwaite and is played with real relish by Val McLane. A remarkable parody of Margaret Thatcher, it's a move which simply wouldn't happen on modern children's TV, hinting at how much the world has lost touch with politics in recent years.

A warmer take on adult authority is the eloquent Whistle Willie, but the main reason for his popularity with the students is down to him being a pushover. Ken Jones, of course, is a fine performer with great comic timing, so benefits from the extreme lengths Willie is pushed to.

The absolute star of the show is Tony Slattery. Bursting with comic smarts and all the confidence of an actor on the way up, Slattery takes on the challenging multi-personalities of Joe Winter and manages to nail each one effortlessly.

The narrative awaiting each character differs wildly

depending on the series that they appear in. The first series' reliance on its sketch format and pop star appearances give it more of a variety feel, but the second series foregoes this and feels more like a sitcom, albeit a musical one. They're not *exactly* different shows, but they feel diverse enough that it's impossible to declare one better. Whilst the first series has Fanshawe and contemporary pop stars popping up, it doesn't have Tony Slattery or a superb parody of Margaret Thatcher lighting up the screen. And vice-versa.

What both series have, in absolute spades, is a scintillatingly anarchic sense of comedy and an incredible set of songs.

Sure, some of the gags are groan worthy, but there's a joy in their cheeky delivery, most notably from Chas and AWOL. We also get Paul performing his irreverent take on *Newsround,* an excuse for plenty of quick paced gags and, just to confirm its comic backbone, a custard pie splatting.

Fanshawe, of course, remains disturbing whenever he appears on screen, but his dedication and subservience to the sacred school dinner is a stroke of surreal genius. And then there's the one man rampage of GBH and his delightfully blunt epitaph of "Here lies Fred Sprout, over and out".

It's not just the children capable of creating laughs, the adults manage to conjure up more than a few as well.

Joe Winter, of course, is a comedy masterclass from Tony Slattery, all intelligent, confident and supremely silly at the same time. It's a difficult combination to pull off, but whether he's suffering mental anguish in Mega Pig's office or preaching love and peace, Slattery achieves it like a pro.

Mega Pig and Braithwaite's contempt for their pupils may feel Dickensian at times, but it's shot through with such a measure of cartoony malice that it's difficult not to revel in their glorious nastiness.

The songs, meanwhile, are swarming with magnificent lyrics about anarchistic ankles, sucking up to parents and the culinary delights of Trolley Molly. Perfectly burrowing into the subversive mindset of schoolchildren, there's little more you can ask for in terms of theme.

What's really special about the songs is that they're packed with a uniquely British flavour, one that feels a world away from the polished seriousness of *Fame*. After all, how often did *Fame* perform songs about the love between a Margaret Thatcher facsimilie and her pet python?

End of Term Report

It's very easy to be wary about musical comedy due to the intricate skill required to fuse the two genres together successfully, but *Behind the Bike Sheds* makes a strong case for not hunting this genre to extinction.

Not only is the comedy and music of a level capable of tickling your funny bone and pricking up your ears, but there's much more going on in this entertaining melee. From the gothic horror of Fanshawe through to the biting parody of Mega Pig, it's quite unlike anything else.

Ultimately, *Behind the Bike Sheds* was miles more entertaining than anything I saw unfolding outside the window of my French lessons. Sure, it wasn't a realistic representation of school life, but that, after all, is the escapist genius of TV.

OVER THE MOON

BBC1
1978

Science is a wonderful pursuit and one which allows mankind to make all sorts of advances to improve our lives. Take this book, for example, it's written on one of those electronic laptops; full of wires, magnets and dilithium crystals, it simply wouldn't exist without science.

However, believe it or not, but science is capable of so much more than providing a nostalgic fool with the means to write about ancient children's TV shows. Instead, one of its primary aims is to explain the world around us and how we can exist in it.

And I've always considered science to be very useful for children getting to grips with the world. Sure, it explains why you can't do really fun things like walk on the ceiling (unless you're a fly), but it also teaches you really cool things like mixing bicarbonate of soda with vinegar.

It's crucial that you keep things fun as children are highly suspicious of any overt attempts at forcing education on them and soon bail out. Therefore, if you can wrap all this studious learning up in layer upon layer of fun, then you'll find yourself with a child who's *Over the Moon*.

Let's Get Learning

Studio bound, but equipped with an array of props to carry out experiments and a generous helping of Chroma key magic, Sam Dale has a brain bursting at the seams with scientific know-how and he's on a one man quest to share this with the curious young viewers at home.

Sam Dale isn't *completely* on his own, though, as a rather bizarre coathanger/question mark hybrid character pops up in the opening titles. After this, his presence is severely limited to that of an emblem on a spinning wheel used to introduce the songs.

Nonetheless, even without a glamorous lab assistant, Sam Dale is keen to use his initiative and scientific savvy to teach the viewers about a wide range of scientific concepts.

Balancing sticks and raindrops are employed to highlight the random hit and miss of chance, the deceptive patterns of snakes and insects provide the lowdown on camouflage whilst the difference between a stone ball and an inflatable ball helps to explain the taxing world of mass.

Eager to emphasise these themes, *Over the Moon* gets the young viewers engaged by providing simple examples of things to do at home e.g. sprinkling ripped up paper over card covered in glue to create random patterns or that old favourite of rubbing a balloon on a jumper to explore static.

Helping the viewer to get more of an impression of these themes in action, stock footage is interspersed throughout the episodes of, for example, spacemen defying gravity in their spaceships and the sky based beauty of creating jet stream trails.

And, bringing another facet of knowledge to the series, *Over the Moon* bolsters its educational arsenal by serving up a musical story with each episode; the animated songs are provided by a whole host of stars such as Jasper Carrott, Carol Leader, Don Spencer and Derek Griffiths.

Again, these songs tie in with the episodes' themes; Jasper

Carrott's 'Angus McBluff' follows the fortunes of a wildlife photographer failing to camouflage himself and Carol Leader's 'The Archer's Arrow' looks at an arrow's flight involving many random misses on its way to an eventual hit.

Aiming for the Moon

Over the Moon was a 13 episode series which first aired towards the end of 1978 on BBC1 in the lunchtime slot. Given the era and the place in the schedules, it's no surprise to discover that it was devised and written by Michael Cole *(Bod, Bric-a-Brac, Fingerbobs)*.

Cole's studio based science extravaganza was directed by Martin Fisher *(Play School, Dizzy Heights, The Quack Chat Show)* who also wrote some of the episodes. Meanwhile, the theme tune – all synths and guitar licks – was performed by the vocal talents of Kim Goody *(No.73, Playdays)*.

Central to the show's appeal were the illustrations behind the songs which were provided by a variety of animators. Alan Rogers *(Pigeon Street, The Flumps)* provided several, Leo Beltoft *(Mr Benn)* pitched in with a couple while Trevor Bond, Mirek Lang and Anna Fodorova produced the rest.

For Alan Rogers, it was the start of an animation technique which would go on to define his career:

"I was working for the Chiswick based animation company, David Yates Ltd at the time. I knew Mike well having worked with him on Bod and the Flumps. Over the Moon came out a few years before I designed and directed Pigeon Street, which Mike also wrote. I remember being asked to animate four songs and it was around the time that I had started to dabble with the "Cut-Out" animation technique, the

beginnings of a lifelong obsession. It was a relatively cheap technique since it wasn't as labour intensive as cel animation.

Not only did this fit in with the low budgets of the BBC children's department, but I also personally loved the look and stylisation. Anyway, I had met Danish animator Leo Beltoft - who later set up King Rollo Films – and we had made a couple of short films together. So, when "Over the Moon" turned up, I decided to use the Cut-Out technique and work with Leo again.

I often animated characters designed by other artists, but Over the Moon allowed me to design the characters myself and experiment with a technique that went on to give me my living.

Traffic Jam Sam was inspired by Mike's son Sam, though I don't think I did a caricature of him. I seem to remember I gave him ginger hair, which the real Sam didn't have. My favourite was Obadiah Blank which was more surreal. It was sung by Derrick Griffiths, who had previously done the music for Bod"

And *Over the Moon* holds a particularly curious position in the history of British children's TV as it was the final original show to debut under the landmark *Watch with Mother* banner. Repeats of the series later aired in the See-Saw slot, with the final episode going out in June 1982.

Unfortunately, out of the 13 episodes produced, only three are known to exist in their entirety due to the 1993 junking exercise which led to many children's TV shows being wiped. One episode 'Whole and Part' is completely missing whilst a further nine episodes are incomplete.

Analysing the Science

Science was one of my favourite lessons at school, so I'm

always intrigued to discover the various ways that this glorious subject can be taught. As with all learning, it needs to be engaging and not veer too close to uninspiring dirge.

And *Over the Moon* particularly appealed to me as it promised science with the added bonus of featuring some of the very best stars of children's TV. With little prompting, I was soon on my way to the BFI Archive.

Down at the BFI, I was able to watch the remaining three episodes: Now You See It, Now You Don't, Hit and Miss and What Goes Up, Comes Down. Would these episodes be as exciting as dropping caesium in water? Or would they be as dull as the periodic table?

As he's the main focal point of the series, it's a good idea to start by taking a look at Sam Dale's role. Still relatively early on in his career, Dale gives a solid performance at the head of the show and – resplendent in 70s fashion – he has the air of a trendy college lecturer.

Dale's main role is to showcase the wonders of science, so we see him harnessing the power of blue screen to camouflage himself against a backdrop of leaves, dropping objects from the same height to examine gravity and attempting to draw circles with his eyes shut to visit the world of chance.

It's not degree level science by any means, but despite the simplicity on offer, I couldn't help but think it was rather advanced for the under 5's. At times it felt more like a particularly chipper BBC Schools programme for the 5 – 7 age range.

Cleverly, *Over the Moon* is mindful to ensure that the more taxing elements of science are cushioned by the presence of some quite magnificent songs; the performers are an eclectic bunch being made up of children's TV stalwarts, soprano Barbara Courtney-King and Jasper Carrott.

Absorbing to the nth degree, it's these songs which solidify the learning on offer and implant the scientific concepts into the young viewers' subconscious. The pick of the bunch are Carrott's accordion led Angus McBluff and Derek Griffifths' jaunty ode to genius inventor Obadiah Blank.

Also worthy of a special mention is Barbara Courtney-King's gleefully absurd tale of Jonathan Jim's problems with gravity that leave him and his neighbours floating a few feet off the air – it's where the answer to life can, apparently, be found.

You know you're dealing with something special when Alan Rogers comes on board, so the songs featuring his animation – such as Angus McBluff and Obadiah Blank – come with that extra frisson of excitement which monopolises your attention and joy.

In between the songs and science, there are the activities for children to try at home and further reinforce the episodes' themes. To 21st century eyes, they're very quaint and would likely have modern children shuddering in fear at the lack of technology involved, but surely the magic of glue and paper, like science, is timeless?

Dark Side of the Moon?

Over the Moon may not be the most spectacular science show, but given the available budgets at the time, it's an admirable attempt to work around this hurdle. As with all good children's TV, the series invests heavily in simplicity and this helps to nullify any budgetary shortfalls.

It's a series which is boiled down to those key constituents of childhood: fun and curiosity. And it's these fundamentals of the developing mind which allow the viewer to pave over the no frills approach which occasionally blights the show.

As a gentle introduction to science, it benefits greatly from big, visual experiments which unravel the many strands of science at a manageable pace. And, crucially, the very high standard of the songs helps to elevate *Over the Moon* into a very special show indeed.

It may be a show which slightly erodes that naive sense of childhood imagination, but consequently, it also imbues children with a new take on the world, one that is grounded with the confines of reality, but just as capable of provoking awe and wonder.

RAGDOLLY ANNA

ITV
1982, 1986 - 87

Dolls find themselves with a fairly limited set of career options. Most are demoted to being dragged around by little girls who take great delight in making the doll wet itself in order to fulfil their maternal instincts.

The only alternative to this life is equally depressing in that it involves being trapped within display cabinets in the garish front rooms of fifty-something women. Neither option is particularly empowering, so it's no surprise to discover a doll trying to eke out a more fulfilling existence in *Ragdolly Anna*.

It's a Doll's Life

Ragdolly Anna lives on the third floor of a flat with the little dressmaker (Pat Coombs). It would seem rather ridiculous to have just these two rattling around in such a huge space, so they're joined by a couple of other characters.

Admittedly, a mute dressmaker's dummy is rather lacking in even the basic definition of character, but it still acts as a sounding board for the little dressmaker. The final entity in the flat is the wise white cat who appears to be of advanced years given his wisdom and cranky temperament.

Episodes focus around fairly simple premises such as Ragdolly Anna popping down the allotment to get on with some gardening. It's a charming enough look at the world of gardening, but there's still room for some whimsical magic when Ragdolly Anna strikes up a friendship with a chatty scarecrow.

And there's a real sense of wonder to be explored in the world that Ragdolly Anna inhabits such as episodes which focus on going to the fair, looking after a giant sunflower and inviting a clockwork elephant round for tea.

The Story of a Doll

Ragdolly Anna started life as a series of stories written by Jean Kenward, but it was the involvement of famed children's TV producer Anne Wood (*Roland Rat, Pob* and *Teletubbies*) which proved to be the spark needed to transfer it to the small screen.

A total of 30 episodes aired over three series between 1982 – 87 on ITV and were produced by Yorkshire Television. Doug Wilcox – who had previously worked with Anne Wood on *The Book Tower* – directed episodes along with John Allen who had also directed episodes of *Puddle Lane*.

Despite the show's narrative simplicity, *Ragdolly Anna* was keen to embrace technology to bring the stories to life. The innovative use of chromakey allowed an actress (Michele Davidson and Caroline Berry) to be shrunk in a Ragdolly Anna costume and then superimposed over the action. When the show wasn't trying to push the boundaries in a CGI-lacking world, they were content to rely on a mixture of live action and static photographs to tell the stories.

The outside locations required for this action to unfold against were situated in Leeds. And to be precise, the tenement flats which were the base for *Ragdolly Anna* were located on Woolman Street. By the 1980s, these flats had fallen upon tough times and in no way reflected the gentle pursuits of *Ragdolly Anna*. The flats have long since been pulled down.

Much like the destruction of these flats, there's little trace left of *Ragdolly Anna* in the modern world. Only a couple of snippets of the show exist on YouTube and this scarcity is down to a lack of commercial releases. This is particularly strange as the show proved successful enough to be sold overseas and even aired on Malaysia TV under their Channel 5 remit.

Dolls Aren't Just for Girls!

I'll be honest; I wanted a doll when I was a lad. It's not an unusual phenomenon in small boys, but this is usually due to their biology kicking in late. For me, it felt different. It was more a fascination with the endearing qualities of a well-crafted doll. And Ragdolly Anna had this in spades.

You see, she's a doll out of time, not just in her Victorian appearance, but also her innocence compared to more sophisticated dolls hitting the shelves in the 1980s. Even back then I had a strange affinity with the past, so *Ragdolly Anna* really resonated with me and felt like a world I never wanted to leave.

Unfortunately, as previously stated, there's barely any footage online, so it was difficult for me to get a more informed and updated perspective on *Ragdolly Anna*. Thankfully, this provided me with an excellent excuse to hop on the train to London, visit the BFI Archives and watch a few episodes. On this particular occasion I booked into watch 'Ragdolly Anna Gets Lost', 'Ragdolly Anna and The Scarecrow' and 'A Visit From Clockwork Elephant'.

It doesn't take long for the charm extravaganza to kick in thanks to the show's fabulous theme tune. It's a delicious slice of rolling music hall piano which is beefed up by brassy horns; the jaunty vocals of Allan Taylor help transform it into a joyous tune akin to Ray Davies and Syd Barrett at their storytelling best.

And as the dying chords of this melodic beast fade out, the narrative begins against a background infused with a familial vibe. Ragdolly Anna is the child of the piece, the little dressmaker is the slightly barmy aunt and the wise white cat is indicative of a wizened grandfather (and what grandfather doesn't have whiskers?).

It's a neat trick to engage with young children for whom family is their moral and social bedrock. They can easily identify with all the familial roles portrayed in Ragdolly Anna, so this provides a comforting crutch to support the interest of not just girls, but also boys.

This recognisable setup is welded to plots from the school of simplicity, but also laced with a curious whimsy to convey a healthy sense of morality. Take, for example, the episode 'Ragdolly Anna Gets Lost' which is the epitome of the show's tone. It starts remarkably twee and mundane with Ragdolly Anna heading to the shops, but then she falls down a drain.

And following this, in true anthropomorphic fashion, a talking frog comes to the rescue. Ragdolly Anna's escape from the dank drain on the back of the frog is an eccentric image, but one which also carries a clear message on the importance of benevolence.

Attempting to bring a level of normalcy to these plots is Pat Coombs. Best known for personifying deferential characters, *Ragdolly Anna* allows her the opportunity to bring more confidence to the table as the little dressmaker. She's a calming anchor of security which helps shore Ragdolly Anna from her slightly more surreal exploits and Pat Coombs' narration brings an enveloping sense of maternal comfort to the adventures.

Raggy Doll?

The innocence of *Ragdolly Anna* still makes for a captivating watch. As I became reacquainted with the show, I found myself as enthralled by its simplicity as I was back in the mid-1980s. And, for the second time in my life, I simply didn't want to leave this world, but circumstances, again, didn't permit me to stay.

Nonetheless, there's a timeless nature to the show's familial narrative which makes me feel it could delight a whole new generation of children. In fact, a Ragdolly Anna toy would be very successful due to its 'less is more' charm; I'd buy one, after all, I've always wanted one.

ZOKKO!

BBC1
1968 - 70

Back in the late 1960s, the mere concept of an electronic comic was laughable. In the 21st century, of course, we're blessed with tablets which can quite easily hold an e-comic. In those swinging sixties, however, I guess the best you could hope for would be a piece of thick plastic with line drawings on and illuminated by a smattering of red LEDs.

Actually, that sounds like a magnificently retro helping of comicabilia and something that I would snap up at auction in a heartbeat. Unfortunately, with just one page, it's not a comic. And it never existed...

That there television, though, it's electronic, right? In amongst all the telly waves and cathode rays there's definitely an electrical source as I've seen the plug. This certainly opens up the possibility of somehow getting a comic on TV and satisfying not only the criteria of being a comic, but also shifting from one section to another without endless stacks of unwieldy plastic and the emotionless red glow of an LED. And a TV version is exactly what you'll find in *Zokko!*

Noise! Adventure! Glitter!

The first incarnation of *Zokko!* features a talking pinball machine which serves as the presenter and helps to link the various features together. With the pinball launched, it soon strikes a hit and the corresponding score indicates a particular feature by announcing, for example, "Zokko! Six!" before launching animated sci-fi serial Skayn.

The first series is much more than just a helping of sci-fi as the myriad features include clips from Disney cartoons, endless children's gags, guest performers such as Davies and Gray with their comedy dance routine and also a "thrill spot" which takes viewers on hair raising adventures via rides on the wall of death and water-skiing.

By the second series, the talking pinball machine has gone and the main links are provided from a studio featuring a collection of test tubes filled up with bubbling liquid. Although the pinball machine has departed, its electronic voice remains and presents similar features to the first series.

This time round the fun includes another helping of serial Skayn and, once this has finished, new serial Susan Starr of the Circus, more Disney clips, specially produced music videos for contemporary songs such as Finchley Central by The New Vaudeville Band, groan inducing gags told over animations and performers appearing include Ali Bongo as the Sheik of Araby and The Tumblairs on their trusted trampoline.

Charging Zokko!

Zokko! was devised and produced by Molly Cox and Paul Ciani with 26 episodes making up the two series between 1968 – 70. Episodes lasted 20 minutes each and both series aired in the Saturday 12.25pm slot on BBC1.

Speaking to the Daily Mirror in 1968, then BBC1 controller Paul Fox explained – with a side slice of contemporary sexism – that the show's timeslot was the perfect way to keep the children busy whilst Mum prepared lunch.

Although the first series of *Zokko!* was repeated in a Wednesday afternoon slot shortly afterwards, the second series was not afforded this luxury and has not been seen publically since its initial airing.

Perhaps the most eye catching aspect of *Zokko!* was the talking pinball table which was designed by Mike Ellis – one of the parents of British entertainment being the father of Blue Peter presenter Janet Ellis and grandfather of pop star Sophie Ellis-Bextor.

The voice of Ellis' construction was provided by another linchpin of British culture in the form of Radiophonic Workshop's Brian Hodgson who also engineered the distinctive TARDIS sound in *Doctor Who* and the Daleks' modulated voices.

Remaining in the audio world for a moment longer, Brian Fahey composed the brass heavy theme tune for *Zokko!* and this was later released as a single by Columbia Records.

Unfortunately, as with so many TV shows of the era, *Zokko!* was almost, but not completely, wiped out of existence from the BBC archives. Although not *quite* having the gravitas of a Stalinist purge, it had a devastating effect on the long term legacy of *Zokko!* as only two episodes of the final series remain in the archives and, for now, the only reminder of the pinball machine is a solitary image which surfaced many years ago.

Flicking Through the Pages

By the time I had emerged from the womb, blinking in the harsh light of a world with only three TV channels, *Zokko!*

had long since finished and it's dire archival status meant I certainly wouldn't be catching it anytime soon.

It was regularly cited to me, though, as a show which deserved my attention. And it's not hard to see why as, despite it having been barely written about, let alone viewed since 1970, the people who originally watched it still have such fond memories about the show. Many of these memories are a little dusty, so I decided it would be a good idea to grab a duster and polish these up, by which I mean: go to the BFI Archive.

Naturally, with series one being completely lost to the ravages of BBC policies, I was unable to get a taste or flavour of this incarnation of the show aside from the aforementioned still of the pinball machine. Luckily, I gained access to the remaining footage of *Zokko!* and this provided me with the chance to view one of the real oddities of British children's TV.

Many people regard *Zokko!* as the inaugural entry in the vast lineage of Saturday morning children's television. However, a few months before *Zokko!* aired, the same time slot had been home to *Whoosh!* starring Rick Jones, Dawn McDonald and Jonathan Collins; far from sharing the same genome as Saturday morning children's TV, though, *Whoosh!* was a very different proposition.

Rick Jones informs me that it was based in an imaginary central headquarters with pneumatic message delivery tubes everywhere. The series had a strong emphasis on comedy and the Radio Times listed *Whoosh!* as a place where anything can happen.

Zokko! also appears to be a place where anything can happen, but it's much more in touch with those later Saturday morning shows than *Whoosh!* And, despite the fact that *Zokko!* never aired on a Saturday morning (only early Saturday afternoons), I'm willing to overlook this as it's a distillation of mostly everything which followed in its wake.

Sure, it's missing pop star phone-ins, competitions and puppet sidekicks, but it also contains DNA which is so readily associated with its kin: animations, music videos, guest performers and all linked together from the comfort of a central set.

And the content which constitutes this now recognisable setup is an intriguing collection of short bursts of creativity and excitement. Short is easily the best word to describe the features contained within *Zokko!* as they fly by at such high speed it's as if *The Fast Show* have commandeered *Live and Kicking* for a morning.

Perhaps the world wasn't ready for a three hour Saturday morning bonanza in the late 1960s, but it's hardly a great loss as the relatively brief running time for features (they're lucky if they stretch over a minute) allows *Zokko!* to have a zippy freshness not usually associated with children's television from the same era.

With the sedateness of its contemporary rivals challenged, is *Zokko!* just a hyperactive collection of visuals or is there some genuine worth in there? Well, after viewing the scant remnants of the show's back catalogue, I can confirm that, yes, it's an exhilarating ride overflowing with curious features.

Naturally, I can't comment on the first series, but I will say that the abstract skull which features on the pinball table is a chilling concoction and, coupled with that electronic droning voice, would make a fine *Doctor Who* villain, albeit one which was even less agile than those pepperpot Daleks.

Moving onto the second series, the set is a good starting point to begin examining the essence of *Zokko!* as its bubbling, oversized test tubes and bright, wildly flashing lights are very much a visual representation of the series' direction. It's an outlook which is highly indebted to the experimental pop culture that it was born into and acts as an arresting spectacle that captures the attention.

The content that follows, not surprisingly, isn't the televisual equivalent of Tomorrow Never Knows and is, in fact, fairly traditional children's entertainment, but it's shot through with a comic flair and a unique packaging to differentiate it from any of its peers.

Sure, the aerial acrobatics of The Sisters Inaros may feel a little bit *too* light entertainment, but this is counterbalanced by the superb silliness of The Hanco Bros who are a slapstick infused circus duo keen on tumbling toupees and cream pies.

Likewise, the space politics of Skayn and big top crimes of Susan Starr (the longest sections at around two minutes) are much more mature than sketches such as the Indian snake charmer who struggles to charm his snake out of the basket without his turban or robe flying skywards. This combination of normality and absurdity could easily become bewildering, but here it plays out seamlessly and displays a fine understanding of the edit suite.

The Disney clips feel like filler material, but you have to remember that this is an era when children's films weren't played out endlessly and would have offered a brief snippet of Hollywood which was usually the preserve of Saturday morning cinema. Much more homegrown, of course, are the animated gags that feature as brief interstitials.

At first I felt that these were God awful groaners, but then it's revealed that around 4,000 jokes had been sent in by children for the second series, so it's difficult to be too harsh on the beloved playground jokes of schoolchildren. This joke, however, had me rolling my eyes at its lack of comedic sense or point:

Knock Knock!
Who's there?
Jack!
Jack who?
Jackanory!

The gags may be corny, but they're married to quirky animations featuring kipper tie and flare wearing chaps (with barnets last seen on Rodney Bewes circa 1974) who lark around opening doors to reveal knock knock jokes, twizzling their moustaches or even just clambering all over the exclamation mark from the *Zokko!* logo.

They're brief, dispensable sections, but fit in with the fast paced ethos of the series and the animations are so indicative of the era that you can almost smell the Brut dabbed on to the animator's neck. And the strongest clue to the show's age comes in the music videos.

These are no ordinary music videos, though, as they're specially shot films for pop songs of the day. Georgie Fame's infectious toe-tapper Get Away, for example, translates into a fairly literal video where a couple of hip, swinging kids jump in a convertible and escape the city folk for a day. And The New Vaudeville Band's chirpy Finchley Central – awash with copious brass and whistling – again goes for the literal by filming a video in amongst the goings on at a London

Underground station.

They're simple affairs, but much more imaginative than just pointing a camera at a miming, disinterested band and sum up exactly why *Zokko!* is such a unique show.

Page Turner?

Given the rich history of Saturday morning children's TV which followed its wake, *Zokko!* deserves to be recognised as a landmark piece of British television for sowing the seeds which would germinate into such a long lasting legacy.

Paul Ciani revisited the *Zokko!* format later in 1970 with Ed Stewart starring in *Ed and Zed!* on Saturday afternoons, but it would take a few years of tinkering until *Tiswas* and *Swap Shop* perfected the formula. *Zokko!* remains an exciting starting point and, like all the best stars of the 1960s, refused to rest on its laurels and, instead, pushed the genre forwards with its brave new vision.

GET UP AND GO! / MOONCAT & CO

ITV
1981 - 85

Even the most experienced of us find the simplest aspects of life a strange affair, so, combined with the number of us humans rushing around from place to place, navigating our way through this tumultuous landscape could easily appear impossible to someone looking in from the outside.

Just take the number of shops down your local high street, every single one of them has a purpose and it's a function we've learned over time e.g. you know to buy your eggs from one shop and your electric drill from another shop. However, we're certainly not born with this knowledge and, with our minds as blank canvasses, we have to gradually piece together how the fabric of the world is woven together, otherwise we'll try and drill holes with eggs.

For an alien visitor, matters are more complex. There's no prior experience to draw upon, so the habits, cultures and emotions of Earth's inhabitants must result in an exponential sense of bewilderment – just imagine trying to explain the phenomena whereby a sock *always* goes missing in the wash.

In fact, a popular exercise set by school teachers is for their pupils to describe an activity in extreme detail for an alien who has descended from the skies. Whilst this is restricted purely to the imagination, occasionally an alien does come down to Earth and their curiosity is more than eager to *Get Up and Go!*

Down to Earth

Leaving his home planet of the moon and descending down through the Earth's atmosphere, Mooncat (operated and voiced by David Claridge) has arrived on Earth to find out more about its inhabitants. Being a newcomer to the planet and its curious ways, Mooncat can't exactly live on his own, so he sets up home with Beryl (Beryl Reid) and Stephen (Stephen Boxer) who help to guide and entertain him with stories and music.

Mooncat has also brought along some of his moon technology, namely the Moon Machine which allows him to peer through either a circle, square or triangle window to monitor those who dwell and toil on Earth. Oh, and he can teleport too.

Looking through the colourful windows of the Moon Machine, Mooncat finds himself examining the life of a window cleaner, investigating where the milkman gets his milk from (to ensure that Mooncat can enjoy his beloved Cornflakes), watching a father and daughter take a trip to the library to borrow some books and even delving into horticultural matters by checking out time lapsed footage of mushrooms and plants growing.

Mooncat doesn't want to limit himself to being a mere observer, though, so he's soon cleaning windows with Beryl or trying to grow plants by planting dolly mixtures.

Helping to back up these dissections of life on Earth, Beryl and Stephen read stories to Mooncat which centre on the adventures of the little girl Billie and her animal friends Woodley the dog, Monkey, Mrs Pinkerton-Trunks the elephant and Mr Milford Haven the lion.

Reinforcing the episodes' themes, these short stories see Billie and the animals panicking about the arrival of a man with a ladder (or 'a lamb with a madder' as Monkey mispronounces) who's actually just a window cleaner and an even more simpler setup where Billie and the gang grow some plants (one of which is named Dorothy Perkins).

Eventually, Stephen moves out of the shared house and goes to work at a local playgroup, but he still manages to find time to visit Beryl and Mooncat every week. Life with Beryl can't go on forever and, fulfilling one of his lifelong dreams, Stephen opens a second-hand shop along with Mooncat in *Mooncat & Co*.

Helped by a never ending stream of customers such as Pat Coombes, Wilf Lunn and Patsy Rowlands, Mooncat continues to learn about the ways of the world by looking into telling the truth, the pain of missing friends and trips to the opticians. The final series of *Mooncat & Co* finds Stephen's brother Berni (Berni Flint) taking over the shop whilst Stephen is away buying stock.

Get Up and Start Filming

Get Up and Go! ran for 56 episodes over three series between 1981 – 1983 whilst *Mooncat & Co* managed two series and notched up 32 episodes between 1984 – 85. Both productions were written by Rick Vanes with Shirley Isherwood and Sally Wells penning the illustrated stories in *Get Up and Go!* and *Mooncat & Co* respectively. Produced by Yorkshire Television, the two shows aired in the lunchtime slot on ITV and repeats followed shortly after each series' initial run.

Rick Vanes had previously worked on scripts for Yorkshire Television and he remembers this association leading to the creation of *Get Up and Go!*:

"Lesley Rogers / Lesley Smith (she used both names during the course of the series) was asked to take over as producer on a long-running series called Stepping Stones, and wanted to put her own stamp on it. Lesley had given me my first break as a writer, allowing me to write a test script for an educational series for deaf children that she was planning.

She liked the script and I went on to write two series of the show, Insight, and so when she was given Stepping Stones, she asked me to write it and come up with some ideas. She wanted it to be entertaining, but full of good educational content for pre-school children, and fancied having a puppet in it.

I came up with a cat from Outer Space, who wanted to find out about life on earth - thereby teaching the viewers at the same time - and named him Mooncat. It was a variation on the name that the early Beatles briefly gave themselves: Johnny & the Moondogs.

My other big idea was that instead of having a young presenter (most pre-school series at the time seemed to be fronted by bouncy young things, often wearing dungarees) we should have a grandma figure. I said my ideal would be Beryl Reid... and everybody laughed. Fat chance!

After my original suggestion of casting Beryl, Lesley Rogers approached her agent. Lesley was utterly charming and persuasive, and managed to sweet-talk Beryl into considering doing it. Lesley, a researcher and I went to have lunch with Beryl at her cottage by the Thames, and by the end of the afternoon she had agreed to do it. I think the clincher was that Beryl was dotty about cats - the cottage was full of them"

Starring opposite Beryl Reid, of course, was Stephen Boxer who remembers securing his place on *Get Up and Go!* whilst playing a role far removed from anything Mooncat ever encountered:

"Get Up and Go! was due to be filmed in Leeds at YTV. I was playing the tetraplegic patient in 'Whose Life is it Anyway?' at Leeds Playhouse. Whether this qualified me for a job as presenter of a children's programme I don't know, but I think our first producer, Lesley Rogers, came to see it, we met and that was it. I was chuffed to get the job, I have much to thank Lesley for"

Integral to the development of Mooncat was the man behind the puppet, David Claridge, who would later go on to create Roland Rat. In fact, it was the rapid and burgeoning fame brought on by Roland Rat which would mean that David Claridge was unable to carry over to *Mooncat & Co*; in his place, puppeteer Christopher Leith stepped in to operate and voice Mooncat.

Going back to the early stages of production, Vanes was highly impressed with David Claridge's talent:

"We spent a whole day in London auditioning puppeteers, without finding anyone who really impressed us. Last on our list was David Claridge, who was appearing on stage in a Mickey Dolenz production, operating a dog puppet, which he controlled with rods while wearing a blackout suit (and remaining in full view of the audience). Because of his theatre matinee commitments, he couldn't make the auditions, so we had arranged to see him in his flat late in the day.

We nearly didn't make it, because Lesley was dispirited and exhausted and tempted to take an earlier train back to Leeds - but I felt we ought to see him, and she agreed. That was a great decision! David gave a brilliant audition, talking to us and operating the dog puppet at the same time. At one stage it even started humping my leg while we were talking about the character of Mooncat - and that clinched it"

By the final series of *Mooncat & Co*, the cast and crew had changed considerably compared to those who had worked on the first series of *Get Up and Go!* as Vanes explains:

"Tragically, Lesley Rogers/Smith died of cancer at a very young age while Get Up and Go! was still running, and an experienced director/producer - Len Lurcuck - took over. The first cast change was Beryl leaving to do Smiley's People for the BBC - a major drama, so who could blame her? Between us, Len Lurcuck and I felt she was a hard act to follow, and it wouldn't really be right to cast an actress to replace her.

So Len and I came up with the idea of Stephen acquiring a shop and getting Mooncat to help him - Mooncat & Co. This would allow us to introduce a rotating cast of characters visiting the shop, in place of Beryl. I can't remember who chose the actors and actresses who featured as visitors and friends - the task was probably just handed to the Casting Dept. And then Stephen Boxer and David Claridge left to do other things. So we brought in another puppeteer and Berni Flint in place of Stephen"

As well as the cast and title changes, there were a number of other slight differences which affected the look and feel of the Mooncat universe as time went on.

The original opening credits for *Get Up and Go!* featured children rampaging round at birthday parties, market stalls and libraries, but this was later replaced by the more familiar animated opening of Mooncat zooming down to Earth in a spacesuit. The first series also found John Sunderland illustrating Shirley Isherwood's stories, but from the second series onwards, Maureen Roffey lent her artistic savvy to the proceedings.

Sending a Man to the Moon(cat)

I was far too young to catch any of *Get Up and Go!* when it originally aired (I wasn't even born until shortly after the second series) and if I did manage to sit in front of *Mooncat & Co* then these memories are lost to that pesky biological phenomena known as infantile amnesia.

However, the more I heard about these two shows, the more I wanted to see them. After all, Rick Vanes has amassed a long list of writing credits and the fact that this includes *The Riddlers* is reason enough to tune in. And, wait, it also features TV legend Beryl Reid? And an up and coming David Claridge? No longer was it a case of wanting to see them, I **had** to see them!

Having never received a commercial release, and the last repeat airing over 30 years ago, tracking down footage of the two series was not simple. Thankfully, the BFI were able to come to my assistance and provided a selection of episodes from across the entire series for me to watch down at their viewing rooms.

Excited by this prospect, I donned my genuine mid 80s Casio watch (I always do this when revisiting the decade's TV) and headed down to London where the streets are truly paved with archive TV – well, a small side street just off Tottenham Court Road at the very least.

Get Up and Go! immediately gets the young viewers on side by making use of a simple, familial setting which is immediately identifiable. Beryl is a dotty Grandmother type character, but one who is shot through with a thespian air and the wisdom this bestows on her underlines her eccentricity with a certain authority.

At a slightly lower position on the age spectrum is Stephen who is like a cool, older brother who can not only play guitar, but also has an immensely likeable boy next door charm.

It's through Beryl and Stephen, of course, that the framework of experience and learning is set down for the star of the show, Mooncat. A cute, astro-cat (he still retains part of his spacesuit as a collar) who is a curious shade of turquoise, Mooncat is clearly meant to reflect the child watching and demonstrates a thirst for knowledge about the world which perfectly reflects the outlook of the young audience.

Prone to shouting out "Hooray!" Mooncat is an excitable feline and has a naïve outlook on the ways of Earth, hence his complete bafflement at concepts such as libraries and housework (to be fair, housework still confounds my natural impulses).

Operated by the enigmatic David Claridge, the puppetry behind Mooncat is crucial not just in affording the character a full range of idiosyncratic movements and expressions, but also in allowing the character to do more in the series. Rather than restricting Mooncat's position to specially built stands, David Claridge focused heavily on the show's production to get the best out of Mooncat as detailed by Vanes:

"David Claridge's drive to push the boundaries of puppeteering was

highly important for the series — for example, teaching us all that the puppeteer didn't necessarily have to hide behind something; he could be in full view of everyone in the studio, but unseen by the viewer because of the framing of the shot, using camera cut-off. That gave us so much more freedom in incorporating Mooncat into the action. I subsequently put that knowledge to good use in The Riddlers, *where we did a lot of outside filming and I was able to script all sorts of fun stunts"*

Together, the fusion of age groups and personalities provided by Beryl, Stephen and Mooncat forge a convivial atmosphere that, like all the best lineups, is built upon fantastic chemistry. Boxer remembers the time spent with his *Get Up and Go!* co-stars fondly:

"Beryl was a comic genius, and going out for supper she could regale us with anecdotes for hours. She had a wicked and at times coruscating wit. Twice married and divorced, if someone annoyed her on sound or elex she'd say 'I've seen off two husbands. I can see you off mate.'

She was also aware of her status, and insisted on there being a 'keylight' for her to hone in on in the studio. All I saw were banks of general lighting, but I was happy to concur. Saying that, there was one take when I came on and stood by her with a 'Good morning Beryl', to which she replied tartly 'Morning Stephen' whilst digging me sharply in the ribs with her elbow thus removing me from her self-styled spot.

David Claridge and I became good friends and shared a house whilst shooting in Leeds. He had the most extraordinary creative imagination ranging from puppetry to pop music (he produced Monsoon's 'Ever So Lonely' amongst others) to setting up a club (Skin Two in central London) and I remember him running the idea for Roland Rat past me ('There's this rat lives in the sewers under King's Cross'), complete with drawings.

> *He could translate his imagination into form too and designed and, I think, made the original Mooncat puppet. He was an obsessive collector of Japanese robots and Transformer toys so my kids used to love visiting him"*

And these hearty relationships are given a further welcome bedfellow in the guise of the *Get Up and Go!* format. The central element of the series is clearly education, but it's one that celebrates a world which, despite being humdrum to the weary eyes of adults, is a never ending sense of awe and wonder to the young audience's eyes.

Take libraries, for example, which adults may view as studious, academic places to avoid, but for children – hamstrung by limited funds – it's a magnificent portal to the worlds of fact and fiction where, get this, you can just take the books away.

The guts of these episode themes are nicely dealt with by the filmed inserts, but this alone would be a meagre offering for anyone watching. Thankfully, *Get Up and Go!* eschews doing the bare minimum and makes sure that a whole package of fun is served up.

That's why we get to see Mooncat tackling these topics with a childlike glee as he writes a rhyming book with Beryl and Stephen, cleans dirty windows and does his absolute utmost to secure a pint of milk following the non-appearance of the milkman.

Solidifying these themes further are the wonderful stories provided by Shirley Isherwood. Whimsical and filled with eccentric characters, these tales embrace simplicity to their very core and contain simple plots such as Mrs Pinkerton-Trunk's lifelong desire to have a rose garden all of her own.

Embellished with Stephen's piano flourishes, these stories are pure nuggets of children's fiction and somehow manage to pack a whole universe's worth of adventure into just a few minutes. They tie in seamlessly with the rest of the program and Vanes remembers a great working relationship:

"Shirley was a factory machinist at the time, but she was trying to make it as a writer for children. Lesley had seen some of her stories and loved them, and championed her work. So she asked Shirley to write stories for the show. How it worked was that Lesley, the researchers and I developed a list of themes for each show (Sharing, Push and Pull, Taking Turns, etc.), I would write the scripts while Shirley was writing her stories, and then I would marry the two together. Shirley was lovely, and she and I became great friends"

Ensuring that there's nowhere for the young viewers' attention to run to, Get Up and Go! pulls one final trick out of its back pocket with a collection of songs that use rhyme and melody to add another layer of learning and, of course, the all-important fun factor. Boxer remembers the songwriting process as enjoyable and still harbours aspirations of pop stardom:

"I wrote about 80 songs over three years to Rick Vanes very smart and witty lyrics. They always suggested a melody to me so, though there was some pressure in terms of time, they were a joy to compose. David and I were constantly badgering the YTV Enterprise Dept. to issue a (then) cassette of the songs but they're still collecting dust in a box in my cellar so I'm open to offers. When I'm feeling Ill / I Wish I Could Whistle as Well as a Bird / I Love Decorating - everyone a sure-fire hit"

Times change and *Get Up and Go!* becomes *Mooncat & Co* with the previously mentioned cast changes. And it's still a splendid show. The loss of Beryl Reid and David Claridge is immense, of course, but their replacements take over faultlessly.

Pat Coombes is the guest presenter in the very first episode and provides a tantalisingly glimpse at what could have been the perfect long term Beryl Reid replacement, but, like many of the guest presenters, it remained a one off appearance. Meanwhile, the noticeable change in voice is a little jarring at first, but Christopher Leith brings Mooncat to life to complete a mostly seamless transition.

The format of *Mooncat & Co* is very much the same as *Get Up and Go!* and the set itself appears to be the same one, but slightly redressed to allow for the shop front and Mooncat's bedroom to become the focal points of the action. Mooncat also introduces Robert the Robot in the first episode 'Shop', a toy robot who chips in intermittently with observations.

There's a further change in the second series as Stephen Boxer departs and Berni Flint comes in as his replacement, but Berni is a marvellous addition and there's a fine chemistry between himself and Mooncat that helps retain the series' soul.

The first Berni Flint episode 'Missing You' looks at Mooncat's angst over Stephen's absence and is surprisingly poignant for a pre-schooler show, but Mooncat soon perks up as he heads to the local train station to visit a photo booth and take a photo to send to Stephen.

Other episodes find Mooncat designing a map for Berni to navigate his way to the post office, Wilf Lunn visits to buy a new hat which he proceeds to pull table legs out of before putting the hat back on and levitating (no, really!) and the final episode sees Mooncat getting a pet rabbit, Ron.

This series proved to be the Mooncat's final hurrah with Rick Vanes feeling that the series had run its course and Mooncat's exploration of our curious little planet came to an end.

Good Kitty?

Get Up and Go! still holds endless memories for a whole generation of children born in the latter part of the 1970s, but more generalised looks at the genre seem to forget it and concentrate, instead, on much longer running shows of the era such as *You and Me* and *Rainbow*.

However, there's a reason that Mooncat managed to maintain a near constant presence on ITV for four years and that's down to the wealth of talent involved. Every aspect is an incredible exploration of what children's TV can achieve in terms of content, acting, production and the cumulative magic that this endows the series with.

There's so much to celebrate about the series – particularly in the shadow of all those cast changes – but most importantly, it's the size of the smile it puts on your face. And it's a worthy reminder as to why children's TV remains in our hearts and minds all these years on.

Acknowledgements

This book wouldn't have been possible without the help of:

The BFI Viewing Service
The BFI Reuben Library
The British Library
Kaleidoscope
Daniel Peacock
Mo Harter
Gordon Griffin
Elsa O'Toole
David Wood
Juliet Lawson
Chris Downs
Kevin Stoney
Simon Buckley
Mike Amatt
Bernard Ashley
Gail Renard
Philip Bird
Sarah Lermit
John Telfer
Tony Husband
Patrick Gallagher
Barry Angel
Elizabeth Lindsay
Rick Vanes
Alan Rogers
Rick Jones
Stephen Boxer
Rachael Clinton
All my Twitter followers

Printed in Great Britain
by Amazon